JEAN LORRAIN

THE BLOOD OF THE GODS

TRANSLATED AND WITH AN INTRODUCTION BY
JACOB RABINOWITZ

THIS IS A SNUGGLY BOOK

Translations and Introduction
Copyright © 2023 by Jacob Rabinowitz.
All rights reserved.

ISBN: 978-1-64525-138-5

Our thanks to Hoffman/Chapman Publishing Services, for assistance in preparing the manuscript.

*It seems a holy thing to mortals,
who are so little better than sacrificial beasts,
the gore that pleases the gods.*

*dedicated to
Leconte de Lisle*[1]

THE BLOOD OF THE GODS

"JEAN LORRAIN" (1855-1906) was the pseudonym of Paul Duval, adopted at the insistence of his father, a Norman ship-owner, who wanted to protect the family name from the disgrace of employment by a poet. A flamboyant homosexual dandy, when forced to make a living from his pen after his father died ruined, he became one of the most prolific and highest-paid journalists of the *fin-de-siècle*, and the personification, in his lifestyle as well as his writing, of the Decadent Movement. *Monsieur de Phocas. Astarté* (1901; tr. as *Monsieur de Phocas*), compounded out of numerous short stories, is a kind of retrospective summary of the Decadent world-view, written after he was forced to leave Paris because of health problems occasioned by his use of ether as a stimulant, which did not take long to kill him thereafter. English translations of some of his short stories are contained in *Nightmares of an Ether-Drinker* (Snuggly Books, 2016), *The Soul-Drinker and Other Decadent Fantasies* (Snuggly Books, 2016) and *Masks in the Tapestry* (Snuggly Books, 2017).

JACOB RABINOWITZ is the author of numerous translations from various languages, living and dead. He is presently editor of the online SF/Fantasy literary magazine *96th of October*.

CONTENTS

Introduction / 13

Prologue / 21

GOLDEN LEGENDS
   Odile / 25
   Heroines / 32
   Enid / 35
   Vivien / 37
   Elaine / 38
   Guinevere / 39
   Melusine / 40
   Isolde / 41
   The Sorrow of King Witlaw / 42
   Captives / 53
   Briseus / 55
   Andromeda / 56
   Andromache / 57
   Ennoia / 58
   Cassandra / 60
   Cressida / 61
   Lorelei / 62

THE PERFUME OF ANTIQUITY
   The Golden Cup / 75
   A Golden Dream It Was / 76
   When I Was a Child / 77

Florence / 78
Apollonia / 80
A Lord's Privilege / 81
Sunt Lacrimae Rerum / 84
The Highway / 85
Forgotten / 87
Horizon / 88
Harold / 89
The Deep / 92
Three Poems for Sully Prudhomme / 94
In the Women's Quarters / 100
For Madame Lacroix / 104
Andrea Foscari / 105
Renaissance / 106
To a Genius / 107
The Swans / 109

THE BLOOD OF THE GODS
Ephebes / 113
Ganymede / 114
Shepherd Boy Alexis / 115
Narcissus / 116
Hylas / 117
Young Bacchus / 118
Bathyllus / 119
Attis / 120
Patroclus / 121
Antinous / 122
Princess Audovere / 123
Ennoia / 126
Love Left / 134
The Gods / 136
Eros / 137
Selene / 138

Zeus / 139
Aphrodite / 140
Apollo / 141

Epilogue / 143

Notes / 147

INTRODUCTION

Jean Lorrain was born Paul Duval at Fécamp, a historic port town in Normandy, on August 9, 1855. His father, Aimable Duval, was a gruff, pragmatic factory owner who produced firearms, and later branched out into lime and bricks.

Lorrain's mother, Pauline Mulat, was of a wealthier, better educated family. Her marriage was not a happy one. Her husband philandered, she found provincial life dull—and so she employed her best energies doting on her only child, Paul.

The beauty of the ocean and of gothic churches, and a profound understanding of the stupefying dullness of rural life—the setting of his childhood—are constant themes in Lorrain's writings, and already evident in this his first book of poems.

His neighbors were the du Maupassant boys, Hervé (one year older than Lorrain) and Guy (five years older.) The latter took a particular pleasure in luring his younger fellows into deserted, spooky places and then leaping out at them with ghostly cries. When Lorrain made his appearance in literary Paris, Guy pointedly distanced himself from his former playfellow, and Lorrain accepted the status quo with icy equanimity.

Lorrain was twenty-three when he finally made it to Paris, after nine years of a simultaneously spoiled and neglected childhood, eight years of boarding school, and five years of idleness at home while he tried to decide what to do with himself—a long lull interrupted by one year of required military service. His father endeavored indefatigably, and without success, to interest him in business. Finally it was decided the young man would study law in Paris. The father envisioned his son embarking at last on a successful career, while the latter thought only of a liberated life in the capital.

This was the bohemian Paris of the Latin Quarter and Montmartre, the Paris of the Impressionists, where an aged and alcoholic Paul Verlaine, still a revered figure, tottered from café to café, and Arthur Rimbaud's writing was gaining ground with the younger generation.

After two unsuccessful years at law school, Lorrain finally persuaded his father to support his attempt at a literary career. Duval *père* agreed—on the condition that he adopt a pen name to spare the family the shame of having produced a poet. Thus Paul Duval became Jean Lorrain.

Le Chat Noir—the famous cabaret, salon, ongoing costume ball and fun-house—had just opened its doors. There Lorrain debuted his poetry and made the acquaintance of the new generation of artists and writers.

It was then that Lorrain began his friendship with Rachilde, the twenty-something cross-dressing authoress of kinky novels, and the recluse painter Gustave Moreau whom Huysman would soon make celebrated. As he made his first forays into journalistic pop-fiction, which he would make his living writing, Lorrain published this, his first book of poetry. His father put up the 500 francs required by the prestigious but pragmatic publisher Alphonse Lemerre. Even then, poetry tended not to sell. The present volume was no exception.

※

Lorrain had a peerless narrative sense, and his poems, as stories, are brilliant. His powers of invention are perverse and startling. Each poem is an intense little episode, evocative of an entire drama. His descriptions have the magical hyper-realism of Pre-Raphaelite painting—they are vivid and instantly appealing as only kitsch can be.

A word should be said here in defense of kitsch. Though the word is generally used as a catch-all term for bad taste, it has a rather specific meaning. Kitsch, properly defined, is predictable, sentimental and over-wrought. It delights us because it gives us what we would like to think, and what we would like to feel, and does so with an explicitness that requires no effort of imagination. Lorrain's bodice-ripping genre-fiction sensibility is purest kitsch. Kitsch can sometimes be great art—and it's almost always great fun.

Further, Lorrain exemplifies homosexual sensibility and taste with a frankness and artistry that would not be matched till the mid twentieth century. If Lorrain had written these as prose poems, his brilliance would have been evident, and he would no doubt have been rewarded with an obscenity trial.

A word is here due about Symbolist, Decadent, and Pre-Raphaelite art, that wonderful nexus of kitsch and over-refinement that we sum up in the term *Fin de Siècle*. This many-named utopia of questionable taste was the final act in the drama of Romanticism.

That movement, which began about 1800 with Bryon and Goethe, was centered on a self-involved gloomy masculine heroism, which found its pattern and prototype in Milton's Satan. The *Fin de Siècle* was the gay reverse of this obverse, and it was dominated by the figure of the Fatal Woman, *La Belle Dame Sans Merci*—a transvestite fantasy without relevance to (or interest in) actual women—whom (be it noted) all the Romantics (Baudelaire is the parade example) despised. The archetype of the Fatal Woman, a self-serving male fantasy about Womankind, extends from Poe's Ligeia all the way to

Theda Bara and the mythologies of early Hollywood. Though it began as a gynophobic myth, by the end of the nineteenth century it had evolved from kitsch to camp, and become a gay male psychological icon.

It is no coincidence that the last gasp of *Fin de Siècle* narrative, the Universal horror films of the 1930's, are a roster of homosexual actors and directors. *The Bride of Frankenstein* is properly the final act of this century-long drag revue.

※

Lorrain is the Baudelaire of *Fin de Siècle* poetry—for the author of *Les Fleurs du Mal* set the style and established the standard for the rest of pre-modern French poetry.

A gay Baudelaire, Lorrain's poems pulse with the erotic shame and the obsessive excitement that sex only acquires from repression. His is the defiance of the instinctual drives, which no moral law can forever restrain.

In his poetic pantheon Lorrain, of course, gives pride of place to his iterations of the Fatal Woman, and these are peculiarly convincing, since they are based on the female figures who he personally adored, not as objects of desire but of emulation—Sarah Bernhardt being the ultimate and somewhat reluctant focus of our poet's adoration.

Among Lorrain's women, none are more poignant and profound than Ennoia, the holy whore of Gnostic mythology, who symbolizes for Lorrain the furtive promiscuity which was for centuries the only expression of gay identity, and the confusion of religious and romantic impulses—the overheated pious sentimentality—that religion always produces when it opposes sex.

We see in the iconic ephebes of this book's final section clear reflections of the mouth-breathing, working-class males

Lorrain was drawn to—because debauchery has no intellectual door policy, and because a certain kind of feminine masochism associates brutish stupidity with "real" masculinity.

These poems are, in their way, more deserving of the title "Flowers of Evil" than Baudelaire's masterpiece. Hothouse blooms from the forbidden Cities of the Plain, impossible orchids—they retain their fascination and only gain in strangeness for our more accepting world.

Indeed, these are more than flowers, they constitute an entire enchanted forest of beautiful, grotesque, cruelly banzai'd desires.

THE BLOOD OF THE GODS

PROLOGUE

I

Birth of a poet. His cradle was draped
in purple and gold. His parents hung
above it a shining lyre
from the branches of a laurel tree in flower,
they laid a long sword against its trunk.

Along came the muse, took the carven lyre,
spurned, with proud foot, the sword to the ground.
Turning to the newborn whose face was wet with tears,
she soothed him with a touch
as comforting as drugs.
In the shade of the tree, her smile flashed,
she murmured these words,

"You will be a poet, with wide clairvoyant eyes,
you'll never lose your astonishment at nature
and thus you'll always live in the golden world,
a laurel wreath on your brow,
a purple robe on your shoulders.

"Pale, your eyes forever scanning the stars,
you'll always be a dreamer, sublime, aloof,
you'll travel by moonlight, mountain streams
will quench your thirst."

PROLOGUE

II

"Shaggy-maned lions, tame to you,
will follow you down the mountains of Greece.
Like them, you'll prowl the crags,
fall asleep at sunrise, the dawn will be your dusk
and days, for you, will be but dreams.

"Satyrs of the forest, pale-skinned nymphs
who live in caves, in the depths of shady valleys,
will stare after you with reverence,
at you who stand on mountain peaks,
drunk with distance, giddy with the winds
that roar along those dizzying cliffs.

"The lips of shepherds and of kings
will open like flowers to disclose the splendor
of your name." So she spoke,
and lifting her arms, bare beneath her blue robe,
save for the golden bracelets
clinking richly at her wrists,

the muse, her head haloed with moonbeams
and sparkling stars, hung the great lyre
at the foot of the exquisite cradle
carved from ivory and pine
(the tree sacred to Dionysus),
in which the infant Orpheus wailed.

GOLDEN LEGENDS[2]

ODILE[3]

I

Stone saints, seated in symmetric series
along the pointed vault, graven angels
of the transept, and the sonorous golden soul
of the bells imprisoned in the tall slender cage
of the belfry tower—all these knew Odile,
as did the poor who crouched shivering
beside the carven balustrade.
So did the clover worked into the pillars,
and the lilies pictured in the windows,
pale blue blooms aglow
through leaden lattice veins;
so did the lamp that shone like a silver star
in the choir's depth—they all knew and blessed
Odile, every holiday and Sunday,
seeing her rosy face and downcast eyes
(blue as periwinkles). When she entered
the dark gothic portal, holding to her heart
her old missal in its ivory binding
with heavy enamel clasps, a freshness
and a warmth as of dawn filled the church,
the clock gave its timely cry
more joyously, ringing out the hour
through the sky towards eternity.

Granite apostles in the church's cave-dark porch
spread their arms in benediction,
looking on her
with their stone and sightless eyes; the angels
standing sculpted along the balconies
in that high vaulted space overwrought with dragons
and bat-winged snakes—those angels seemed to soar
with more enormous assurance;
one could almost hear the roar
of their vast wings on the downstroke,
taking stone immobile flight
across their quarried heaven,
seemingly weightless
and free as sparrows circling in the infinite
azure of a summer afternoon.

Such was the magic that environed Odile,
whose pure soul would have shown
white in the midst of lilies,
for she was no less innocent than they.
The long folds of her dress, though richly woven,
were simple linen, unadorned by any jewel.

Among the proud rich women of the city
who filled the church's aisles with the hiss of their silks
and the jingle of their jewelry, Odile passed,
with unpainted face, through the shadows,
like a Madonna's silhouette.

She gave alms discreetly to the poor at the door,
humbly evaded the gaze of the handsome
young lords ablaze in brocades,
noisy as peacocks and boastful as crows,
toying with their collars of ruby and pearl,

dipping their long and delicate fingers
in the holy water to offer a sarcastic
sprinkle of blessing to the heavy-set
wives of magistrates.

Odile swerved to avoid these fine folk
who stood in her way with arrogant grins,
and headed straight for the ragged beggars
in the square. With pensive sympathetic expression,
she kissed the brows of the sick,
gave them white bread from her own table.

By the basin of holy water,
Saint Mark with his eagle, John with his lamb,
Luke with his dog, seemed to see all she did
and see that it was good.

II

Among those bored young lords, love-hunters
and lady-slayers, laying snares
for unwary demoiselles, appeared Count Horn,
just returned from Rome (where Saint Peter's trustee
led a merry life), bringing with him a company
of Tuscan adventurers, fierce to the weak,
soldiers of fortune whose leers all ladies feared.

Proud of his strength, proud of his breastplate
inlaid with silver, and his gold-embroidered gloves
which he considered far more impressive
than that Madonna with her lilies
in the church window's stained glass,
Count Horn addressed his fellows on the steps,

May the Blessèd Virgin strike me dead
and Saint John flay me living,
if things go on like this. I've stood
and shivered in the shadows of these portals
hoping for a kiss from that pious child
Odile, who keeps us waiting
as though we were her servants.
God's blood, what a joke she's played on us!
I've sat through three masses
with interminable sermons
already today, not to mention confessions,
sitting with my ear to the partition in the hope
of hearing her whisper some dim little sin.
That virtuous brat's made fools of us all!
We forfeit our glory, our reputation
as conquerors—on which so much of conquest depends.

At the duke's yesterday, Madame de Bouillon
raised a laugh that rippled to verge of her circle,
suggesting we needed to hone our skills
by ruining the reputation of a few chambermaids!
So exorbitant's the cost to us
of Odile's virtue. We're hers to play with
like a set of dolls. Instead of us attacking
her virtue like a castle, she leads us like sheep.
What time have we wasted being gallant,
kissing hands—girls don't like to give
what they want you to take.
I know how women's minds work,
and I swear before you all that before this month is out
Odile will kiss my boots, kneel at my feet
and rub her muzzle against my leg
like a hungry cat. You don't believe me?
I don't need your belief, just be witnesses.

When those pious cows have done lowing to the Lord
and that pretty infant simpers out with her missal
at the head of the weakling herd of hypocrites—
may I receive the beating a braggart deserves
if I don't kiss Odile right on the lips,
and if she doesn't thank me! I'll give my blade
with its all-gold pommel, my damascened cuirass
(which all of you envy), my chestnut horse
with its saddle and trappings, to anyone here
who hears this promise and can say a month from now
my vaunt was nothing but words." With a laugh
they accepted his pledge.

Just then the organ's distant roar
marked the end of the mass. The crowd flowed out,
the carillon pealed its joyous din
above the ancient town, filled sky with glad clangor,
and Odile, with snowy neck modestly inclined,
emerged from the pillared shadows. Sweet,
unhurried, she paused to give alms to the lepers
crouching on the church steps. Her blond hair haloed
her face in gold, like a painted saint's.
Heaven shone in her face.

Brutish, chest thrust out
in arrogance and anger, Count Horn rose
before her, took her delicate fingers
in his great hairy hands, squeezed them cruelly
as though to crush them, said, "Your lips insist
on a kiss, like a flower whose sweet scent solicits
the bee." He met her mouth ferociously with his.

His friends, those cynical indecent monsieurs,
howled with glee. The crowd circled round to see,
shocked to tears at the maiden outraged.

She didn't so much as blush, only lifted
her purse, opened it and asked the count,
"Have you nothing better to offer for the poor?"

He who'd jeered now shuddered and staggered with anger,
wide eyes rolling like a fearful delirious
drunk's. His teeth began to chatter,
his fists unclenched, he clawed in his doublet
for money, then deluged with ducats
the virgin's purse! Pale with rage,
trembling, all against his will,
he emptied his embroidered coin-bag into Odile's.
She, with calm and pleasant expression,
went on her way through the parting crowd
that backed off in terror.

Odile turned again, very self-possessed, and said
to the young lords, "Stay and pray." They remained
on their knees on the dirty flagstones, in tears,
elegant gentlemen among the begging lepers.

As the days went by their brocade fell away,
shred by splendid shred. Their knees
poked out through the holes in their silken hose,
shriveled yellow flesh might be glimpsed through their rags.
Their beards grew long and their blackened nails
became claws. Thirty days and a day,
in the company of old folks on crutches, they wept
and prayed, watching over Count Horn in his coma
outstretched underneath the church's great portal.
Every morning Odile walked among them,
held out her hand, asked in her golden voice,
"Have you anything today for the poor, my lords?"

They plucked their gemmy pins, slid off rings,
unfastened heavy neck chains, and gave.

On the Feast of the Holy Apostles
the month was done. Bishop Otto
celebrated mass. Beside him stood the clergy,
before him all the people kneeled.
Odile, in white, led a poor old woman,
blind and toothless, whose each unsteady step
cost her a groan, very slowly to where Count Horn lay,
had her kiss his forehead on behalf of the thankful poor.
Then, with Odile's help, he was able to rise.

She said, "Lord Horn, you should be grateful; after all,
it's thanks to me you'll be keeping your sword
with the golden hilt, the cuirass inlaid with silver,
the velvet-covered saddle and the chestnut horse,
finely bridled, with buckles and bit
and fittings from the goldsmith. They're all still yours
because I kept your promise:
you kissed me in front of all the town
and my reply is to thank you for such an affront."
She bowed to the count and entered the church.

Horn, with ashen face, looked around at his friends
in a row along the wall, and joined his hands in prayer
as he heard the golden bells from their tower
like the choral voice of all the stone saints,
each one from their niche with its pointed arch,
intoning a melodious blessing on Odile,
and proclaiming the victory of Christ. Hearing this,
the heart of Count Horn, then and forever
found peace.

HEROINES

Winsome daughters of dreams,
women with long gold hair,
they stand in a circle on the shore,
their stance commanding, proud.

Queens of legend, queens of love,
noble their brows,
and noble the slope of their breasts,
they've come from the forest of Broceliande
(where Merlin is buried, where Vivien lived),
from many a vanished kingdom.

Blue robes worked with golden flowers
express their tall and slender forms,
and on their long fine fingers
rings flicker with gems.

Their plunging necklines show a splendor
more than mortal, defying time:
the centuries are forgotten, fade,
but these remain, divine.

Isolde, Melusine, Guinevere—
names with the melancholy ring
of a distant horn. On the lips of the poet
who yet remembers them, their names

are sweet as a kiss, unforgettable
as a broken heart.

Their names are an incantation
enchanting back to life
their world of wars, of treacherous loves,
the crash and flash of famous swords
which one reads of in the barbarous
Old French of our epics

The poet is still in love with their glories
which inspired once the harping bards
of ancient Gaul,
even now, the poet yet believes in them
(if only fitfully, for the length of a line),
in visions brief and brilliant
as a lightning flash
in the night of Time.

From their graves in the neglected centuries
these forgotten heroines rise,
shed their shrouds to live again.

Their ghosts,
with the interminable sweetness of a dream,
walk again below those cliffs,
on the beach of Brittany,
in the savage, lurid light of a sunset
insistently yellow and red as fanned embers.

Eerily, as in a lucid dream,
one sees distinctly every pearl in their hair,
the transparent pallor of their faces and hands.

The painter, the poet, peering
into the deep well of a dream
see them as they smile,
as they dance, hand in hand,
these golden haired queens.

ENID[4]

Highlighted by a slanting ray of sun,
seated by the hearth: pale Enid,
daughter of Yniol, the hoary-headed earl.

Enid, exquisite as a silvery blossom—
she pulled the wool between pinching fingers,
fed it to the wheel, smiling beside
the ancient dame, her dozing mother.

A rough gust plucked petals from lily and violet,
flew them through the window to strew the floor,
casting floral ornament
on the faded silk of Enid's dress.
A few petals fell
on the neck of the girl bent over her work
like the weightless brilliant kisses
of invisible spirits.

In the abandoned town half-returned to forest,
in a crumbling castle, overgrown with ivy,
captured by branches, overpowered by flowers,
where blackberry bushes had invaded
the courtyard's broken flagstones,

a girl of twenty, Enid sang as she spun,
sweetly melancholy, dreaming of love,

while a king's son stood unseen at the open window.
Through its pointed arch her picture
had forever taken him.

VIVIEN[5]

Deep in the forest of Broceliande,
forever unseen by the stupid curious eyes
of normal folk, Merlin sleeps to this day,
dreaming as one dreams when drunk with love,
of Vivien, pale, lithe Vivien,
with her heavy tiara of braided gold.

She sings where the hornèd thistle blooms,
where the moss beneath the trees gleams blue-green,
where her delicate feet shine with dazzling pallor
in the green night of deep woods at noon.

Her hair, a fierce red-gold, is so long
it brushes the tops of her feet as she dances
in the shady cool of this private leafy grotto
which now feels lullingly warm
to the old man bemused
by the girl, her movement, her perfume—

she looks at him as she dances, looks long,
and he yields her all his secrets,
as she strokes his bald head
with a whore's practiced hands.

ELAINE[6]

Laid out on an ebony barge
piloted by a solitary steersman,
the Lady of Shallot, her face death-calm
and deadly-pale,
glided along the silver ribbon of the river
winding down to Camelot. He coffin-black boat
was as sad a sight as Lethe's stream
flowing in silence through the world of the dead.

With her golden hair and a dress as white
as the lily her clasped hands held at her heart,
the corpse of Elaine, so pure, so worthy
of love, came to Camelot, asking the king
for justice against the lord who would not love her.

Lancelot, so ungrateful for her gift
of a true heart's first love, when he recognized his own
arms embroidered on the pall draping that dark barque,
and her tresses so long they trailed in the water,

that callous knight realized for the first time
how truly beautiful she was. Now it was Elaine
who was cold and saw nothing,
and he it was who wept.

GUINEVERE

When she finally arrived at the floor of the abyss
to which she'd so long been descending, terrified,
along unrailed spiral steps
down the sides of the pit,
and she saw on the ground the scattered petals
that had once formed the flower
of her honor, and she finally saw her crime
for what it was,

she thought back, in horror, on the passion and the splendor
that were hers, and now she cursed, this adulteress,
cursed the hunger of her own hollow heart
and the thirst of her lips, her shameful craving
that led her here where she lay prostrate,
begging forgiveness at the feet of her king.

Her red hair spread out over the flagstones
of the chapel like a pool of fire,
she writhed in her humiliation,
sinuous even in contrition,
on the ground, in the shadows,
yet, as ever, splendid.

Arthur, softened at the sight
of her plaintive face, her abasement,
her red mane caressing the cold floor,
couldn't bring himself to strike her,
he couldn't help but accept her remorse.

MELUSINE[7]

Lovely Melusine—the glance of her blue-green eyes
was enough to make one drunk. Her superhuman beauty
finally so disturbed the people,
they drove her away.

The gates thudded shut behind her, she wandered
slowly away from the town's tall walls,
her heavy gold bracelets and brocade dress
meant nothing to her now. Big tears rolled
down her cheeks to splash her white bosom,
her red disheveled hair cascaded
down her splendid neck.

She headed back to the land of the fairies,
entered a valley where disembodied voices
were calling her name. Wolves followed after
like loyal pets. When she turned her large eyes
to the owl-flown moony night sky,
her gaze made the scudding clouds
halt in mid-heaven.

ISOLDE

The world's outcry, the censure of the court,
all faded into the distance, Isolde
joined Tristan in a deep and secret wood
where the only tattling heard
was that of the birds.

Happy, casual, without her crown,
she wandered, hair cascading o'er her azure dress,
eyes flashing, drunk with love, intoxicating, lovely,
drinking water from streams that sparkled in sunlight,
biting into ripe fruit offered pleasingly by trees.

Unworried by their sin, without a care for their fair fame,
for what they owed to King Mark and his court
—all of that was forgotten like an April morning's dream.

These two, love's exiles, slept beneath the ancient oaks
and the forest stream lulled them to sleep
with its sympathetic whisper.

THE SORROW OF KING WITLAW[8]

for Victor Hugo[9]

King Witlaw the Bold, Lord of Denmark,
was sad, despite his three hundred ships
of fine white oak, clinker-built, with rivetted
overlapping planks, richly carved
into knotwork monsters—
ships which made him master
of the North Sea and the Baltic,
taking tribute from Iceland, Ireland, the Orkneys.
His eagle banner fluttered over the port
of Arhus, a city bristling with bell-towers,
its harbor planted thick with masts.

Twenty marble colossi, erected by the piers,
viewed, with lofty scorn, the waves,
each one of them a heroic ancestor
of Witlaw's. In the evenings the king would stand
on the terrace of his palace, elbows on the railing,
to refresh with sea breeze
his nostrils sated with incense.
He saw those giant statues standing over his harbor,
like chess-pieces forgotten by giants on the beach,
and he was sad. He sat silent on his throne
before his nobles, feeling the weight
of his ermine and purple. His snowy beard

overflowed his chest, he sighed.
He was eighty-four and without an heir.
Bertrade the Blonde was the last of his line
and she was dying. His own shroud was already woven,
he could see the future as if from his death-bed,
as if he were already a ghost!
His kingdom and his city, his crown, all would pass
into the hands of vassals, his name
extinguished, his glory gone
to where fire goes when fire goes *out*.
He himself now wrote, with trembling hand,
the final lines in the epic of his race.

This night, Witlaw, more gloomy than usual,
was leaning more wearily on the marble balustrade.
He shaped Bertrade's name silently on his lips.
In the fierce ruddy light of a sluggish sunset,
while the shadows of his tremendous forebears
lengthened over the town and reached up the walls
of his castle, to cover all. Suddenly
a horrible figure appeared,
dreadful as the truth and vivid as a dream,
bluish-gray, superhuman, startling,
with the hard knotty muscles of a giant
and the ghastly compacted face of a dwarf.
A seaweed-colored helmet, greenish-gold,
crowned its head, and from his hair
trickled sea-water, and with it came a reek
as of a beached thing rotting. A necklace of skulls
hung heavily across its chest.
Eyes closed, with voice hoarse as waves, it intoned
to the king who stood staring, stupefied with fear,

"Sigur, son of Wotan, son of Ymir, son of Enid,
was tall and strong, with helmet and sword of gold.
In two years he subjugated all the tribes
of Arvor. After him came Cedric the Pitiless.
His was an arm like steel and his
were the first longships to reach the shores of Brittany.
The old Gallic bards still remember his name.
His son, Hastings, brought back a whole people in tears,
captured along the rivers of Saxony.
He made so many slaves that every earl had three
just to hold his mead horn. Hastings had golden-haired
bastards as countless as the golden grains
of sand along the shore. His son Wilfred's exploits,
recited by bivouac fires, yet color
young warriors' dreams. Great were Harold,
Yniol, and Geraint—any two of *their* sons
were worth thirty men such as men are today.
Otto's armies led the heroes of other peoples
prisoners, hands bound behind their backs.
MacCumer was so cruel, the kings of the north
came crawling on their bellies to pledge him fealty
the moment they heard his war-horn calling
famine and terror down on the land.
Great Canute, all by himself,
supplied the subjects of twenty epics.
The night after a battle, they'd see him reviewing
the ranks of the dead, calculating the carnage
of the hideous field, his armor gleaming,
his stallion drenched to the chest in blood.
Ireland was nothing but huts and piddling villages
before the coming of Eric the Black.
He'd seize their warriors by the heels,
swing them overhead and hurl them.
Edryn the Blond was the terror of maidens.

He liked to make them writhe in his grip.
In ten months he took twenty cities
and raped twelve princesses. One, the daughter
of Bela, King of Spire,
he made Duchess of Flanders.
The harps of bards who accepted Christ
split into kindling at the mere name of Odrus
around whose helmet ravens circled,
whose lands were always fertile, their soil
soaked by the blood of his enemies.
Last came your father, Erdor,
worthy of his race, worthy of the snowy peaks
and icy fiords, he was acknowledged from those heights
to those depths as the Caesar of the north.
He deployed his longboats over the seas
like wooden chess pieces. Knights, kings and bishops
were all expendable pawns to him.
These proud remorseless lords dominate
our annals, stare back at us from beneath their horned
and terrifying helmets, their crimes
only make their glory shine the more,
because, for all their ghastly battles,
the treacherous slayings, the violated virgins,
these Viking sea-kings were loyal to the gods.
Priestesses of Odin marched before their chariots
with long blond braids. Harbingers of victory,
the battle-glad Valkyries, who love the clash of battle,
chose the bravest of them, brought them back to Valhalla
to fight forever, daily recreated, daily slain.

"The glory of a people lies in how it keeps faith
with ancestral ways, but since the god from Judea
mixed his blessèd blood with that of warrior folk,
the old gods have turned against the race of Hastings,

laid their curse on Witlaw, the shame of his house.
This is why every night on the terrace
of your palace, built so long ago by pagan kings,
you weep. The Christian god with his bread and wine
can't bring life to your dead or fame to your name.
He found you strong, contemptuous of death,
but today it's death who takes your daughter
by the neck and drags her to the grave,
to bed her as his bride.
Your betrayal of the gods, O Witlaw, has woven
your shroud, and left you sad and sole.
I, the spirit of your race, was sent here to curse you,
but I pity you enough to ask you one last time
to return to the old belief, abandon Christ
and his hateful rites, become another Hastings
and slay his priests! The wrath of your ancestors
is ready to crush you. Revere once more
those who gave them glory, who can give life
to Bertrade your dying daughter. Climb back up
the steps of time!"

Witlaw crossed himself and said to the demon,
"No! Christ is God. Begone." Then he wept.
When he looked up again at the sparkling stars
of that gigantic night, the horrid dwarf was gone,
but he saw approaching him a veiled pale figure,
a dim outline he could barely make out
against the shadows. He mastered his terror
and fearfully peering right at it he recognized—
Bertrade.

Witlaw knew she lay in a distant cloister, dying,
across a mountain, past a valley.
He couldn't comprehend how she came to be here,

standing, alive and smiling, her hair
falling over her shoulders, down to her crossed arms.

"She who is blessèd among women
and the Holy Spirit have sent me here in haste,
dear father," she said in a voice so sweet,
so redolent of heaven, earth trembled to hear it.
"Christ, who knows the darkness in the hearts of kings,
knows why you sit here nightly
on this high terrace brooding, and he says to you,
'No, your race won't die with you,
because you said no
to the Evil One and gave God the victory.

"I come asking your forgiveness, father,
I merited your wrath when I refused the husband
you ordained for me. I lived far from you
in the selfish blessedness of my dovecote
while you, royal eagle, turned your weary flight
tombwards. A coward, I refused
to drink the bitter chalice of marriage.
My heart full of heaven, I buried myself alive
in the cloister. Perhaps you'll forgive me.
Great ancient families don't really need daughters.
Woman is born to be a slave and a prey,
a husband's property. But a son,
with red hair and confident clear gaze,
is born to sustain his race. Women wear
the dress, armor belongs to males;
kings wield the scepter, queens the spindle."

"The Lord has humbled me, brought me low
as easily as I'd bend a reed,"
thought Witlaw as he listened. "How can I have a son?

I'm old and sickly. My daughter's head's been turned
by nuns telling legends," to which Bertade replied,
as though she'd heard his thought,

"Age imposes no limits on miracles.
If God so wills, a virgin gives birth.
Hagar bore a son to hundred-year-old Abraham."

"Either she's lost her mind or I have,"
muttered the king, not seeing
the subtle halo glowing round his daughter's brow.

Placing a pale hand on her father's silver hairs,
she spoke in low tones, "Go back, my father,
in space and time to when your beard was still gold,
back to the cliffs of Arvor on the eve
after your ruinous victory, when bodies
of men and horses were strewn along
the darkening beach. Night hid the silent
battlefield. Victors, defeated,
captives, all had gone, but one forgotten straggler
still staggered, leading his horse by the bridle,
bleeding his life away, drop by drop."

"I remember that wound,"
said Witlaw, "it opened my whole right side."

"The abandoned man stopped
and listened. Not a groan could be heard
from the dying, not a horn
from the forces long withdrawn.
There on the deserted shore of Arvor,
none other seemed to live beneath the dull heavy sky.
But far down the beach he saw a doubtful gleam,

perhaps a lantern warning sailors of a reef,
at the base of the cliff, a lantern with panes
of horn giving faint but steady light.
The wounded one dragged himself along the sands
towards it."

"I see it now," said the king,
"the hut pitched low among the pebbles of the shore,
the fisherman's nets hung up to dry—"

Silencing her father with a gesture, Bertrade said,
"Look inside that thatched cabin,
see the man outstretched
on a bed of dried seaweed. Standing beside him,
raising a copper lantern to see
he breathes easy, a woman is watching over him
with eyes of more than compassionate concern.
How lovely she looks by lamplight, studying
the stranger's noble brow, attentive nurse!
Her husband went fishing down the coast before dawn,
earlier, now that he provides for three—
a serf playing host to the son of a king.
In the hut, someone has blown out the lamp,
the convalescent isn't sleeping anymore;
the woman cries out sharply, like a wounded beast,
but not in pain. The treacherous guest, the guilty
woman, both complicit in this outrage to honor
and trust, a shameful repayment for help
and healing—do you know the traitor's name?"

Closing his eyes to hold back tears,
Witlaw said, "I do."

"Nineteen years have passed,
the shack with the fishnets still stands
on the empty shore. The wounded warrior
left that woman long ago
to her shame and remorse. The good fisherman
died of heartbreak, and the child, disowned
by his father, grew tall. The shore accepted him
as did his reluctant silent mother
for fifteen years, till at last the death
she wished for knocked at her humble door.
The orphan had no one to foster his youth,
just the generous shore,
through which he never lacked food.

"Exploring the borders of his solitary world
he met an old monk of forbidding appearance
but pure heart, who taught the boy to carve
wooden crucifixes. Selling these
he supported them both. Thus the son
of so many kings lives by the kindness
of a hundred-year-old priest, unknown to his father
who thinks himself as poor in offspring
as his own child is in wealth."

Witlaw tearfully rose, hands clasped in prayer
and said, "Can this be so?
Just God makes the high hearts of kings
targets of his well-aimed, well-earned punishments!
So many are the sins covered by a crown
that kings, though bent beneath his displeasure,
don't even know what crime they're atoning for.
The best they can do is fall to their knees
and cry to the Lord, 'My foolish heart
doesn't know what it's done.'

Witlaw stole a fisheman's wife
as David did Bathsheba from loyal Uriel."

The king fell silent, head bowed in shame,
numb with dread, face more gray
before the truth than when the ugly dream
had uttered its lies.

Dawn: the high terrace with its railings
began to gleam, it was bright enough that Witlaw saw,
when he raised his humbled gaze, that Bertrade's lips
were a frightful violet hue, her body was bound
in a shroud, her feet didn't touch the ground,
she floated, seemingly asleep,
immobile in the air,
weightless as a piece of gold leaf.
He knew then that his daughter was dead,
"Bertrade!" he cried, but she'd already disappeared.

Just then a courier entered Aarhu
with the news that Bertrade, Abbess of Saint Edme,
had passed away during the night. That very day
Witaw rode to the cliffs of Arvor,
found the boy carving wooden saints
on the seashore in the old monk's company.
He placed on the lad's head the crown of Sigur
and Hastings. Then the king had proclaimed,
in Saxon and Danish, his sins, his vision,
and recognized his son, Herber, as king.
Then he died. Thus, says the legend,
(which the scribe Gerbert wrote down in the year
one thousand and twenty *anno Domini*)
—thus was established the era
of Christian kings, beginning with Witlaw the Great,

his son, Herber, and his grandson Etienne.
The pagan age, that began with Sigur
was ended by Erdor's son.

As the tomb has his body,
may heaven have his soul.

CAPTIVES

for Theodore de Banville[10]

In the epic poems of the ancient world
a careful ear hears, beyond the ringing of swords
and the crash of shields, the vague
frightened whispering of women.

In their humbled, lowered eyes, one can glimpse
a gleam of hidden hatred,
like a ruddy reflection of Troy in flames
in the hour the war horns sounded
their heartless alarm, their appalling call.

How splendid, the harem-pale bodies of these captives,
their blond unbound hair;
how striking they seem, white highlights
in the red terror of massacre.

Their finely carven belts of gold,
the jeweled bands on their flawless arms,
the dignified sad beauty of their faces resigned
to the cruel commands of Eros!

This one is doomed to be a warrior's prize,
that one's fated to be given away
disdainfully; all are the property of masters,

all will be passed on at last
to be outraged by slaves.

Their bodies are weary of use
and numb to love, their faces have paled,
their features sharpened, their eyes
have become dull and lusterless.

Fading like flowers,
fatigued yet sleepless,
magnificent princesses, daughters
of sunlit shame;

bruised heroines, holy victims,
your disgrace still fascinates.
Imbue these pages with the heat of your feeling,
the troubling perfume of your fame.

BRISEIS[11]

Sixteen years old, with fine blue-violet veins
subtly coloring her noble brow,
sweetly pale as the sky at dawn,
her feet with their opal toe-rings were so delicate
they nearly seemed transparent,
they made one think of a lily's petals
sparkling with dew—

Now she dreams of her girlhood in Lyrnessa,
bathing naked, hidden by the reeds
of the river gliding by the temple
where those bare feet of hers used to dance
on the gleaming stone floors to the barbaric sound
of rattles, drums and cowbells.
Today her ankles are adorned with bangles:
magnificent, yes, but heavy to her.

She thinks she hears again the temple maidens singing
plaintive evening hymns to the darkening sky,
she remembers her vowed virginity,
her neophyte's robes, and, weeping with shame,
she veils her face.

ANDROMEDA[12]

She looked like a lone white blossom
somehow cast upon the shore
to perish on the sun-smit sand,
like an impossible exotic ocean bloom
swept up by a tempest from Poseidon's palace garden.

In the blaze of sunset, the beach glows red as lava.
Shackled to the cliff, her virgin body writhes
as though burned by those figurative flames.
Now the monster swims in with the tide,
a leviathan spouting its triumphant plume of spray.

She moans but can't stop watching.
If she tried to turn her head,
the iron collar would bruise her splendid neck.
Her bosom rises and falls
as she gasps with dread.

She already imagines herself torn and gory
on the strand when, from behind the monster, rises
a horse with wings, its rider the godlike
Perseus, raising his sword.

ANDROMACHE[13]

Seated under the sparkling stars
on the terrace of her palace,
which now belongs to Pyrrhus,
Andromache grins bitterly, recalling all she's lost.
The night wind flutters her veils.

The subtle fire of her woven gold bodice
underlines her splendid bosom.
Her widow's eyes smolder with rage repressed,
softened slightly by the mist of tears
she refuses to weep.

In her mind she sees again the epic career
of Hector, a whirlwind of glory and death,
his chariot racing along the plain
like a wingèd thing.

Brooding on the future, she holds all the closer
the dear small form of Astyanax
who smiles like a little sleeping god.

ENNOIA[14]

Like many another young deity, she wandered.

She couldn't be brought to take the daily
slaughter in front of the gates of Troy
seriously, not a little bit.
Her laughter exasperated even Paris.

But her gaze transfixed men,
like the sight of money, with a golden chain
that was more than a metaphor. Her dainty bare feet
walked on the wounded bodies
of those who had loved her.

When a Greek galley finally brought her back
to Sparta's lush and flowering coasts
a convict bride,
the same indefinable brightness,
that strange and solemn hilarity,
like the eyes of a cat with a human mind,
startled the princes who met her glance.

Since then, she's danced naked on the stage of low dives,
offered her mouth to the red eager lips
of Rome's sturdy porters and suntanned athletes.

The teeth of a Caesar have bruised her bosom,
and in her eyes, red and swollen,
in her dark eyes,
in her eyes of a woman who's been beaten,
the brightness divine, eternal
laughs with inhuman triumph.

CASSANDRA[15]

Heart pounding, her every breath a sob,
weary of daily humiliations,
the priestess Cassandra wanders
beside the green waves. She understands
what the surf repeats,
as she stares out at the ocean's infinity.

The hated embraces of the enemy king,
the home that is no home to her,
the endless subtle snubs every immigrant learns,
are hers, and the lofty scorn of the queen
who hates her—all this darkened her brow
and made her eyes blaze.

She stands on the shore,
in her dress the color of sulfur.
The ocean deeps please her,
inviting her to drown herself and her griefs.

Thoughts of all she's lost filter through her
like the sand grains through her fingers,
like them, she is falling, falling . . .

CRESSIDA

Trojan Cressida had a smoldering gaze,
she breathed in deeply, her nostrils flared.
Her desires never reckoned consequence or cost,
her eyes gleamed green like the ocean waves,
like the ocean waves, they were mobile and cold.

She was pink and perfect and appealing as a cowrie—
so smooth, so soft to the eye, and yet so hard—
kings thirsted for her kisses,
she'd learned the value of those red lips of hers.

She lavished proud smiles on Troy's young warriors.
Hector, Paris, Troilus, all
fell for her, all of them made her moan,

and now she laughed, delighted by the son
of Thetis, flirtatiously she played for him the lyre—
a tender murmuring melody.
Now Achilles, too, was drunk with the virtuoso
brightness of her eyes.

LORELEI

for Leconte de Lisle

I

The guardsmen stood in two lines, halberds in hand,
in baggy knee breeches, noses in the air,
while the rabble and the street kids booed and called
for vengeance on the whore. Inside the town hall
last night's slain were laid out on stretchers,
one of them with twenty deep cuts in his doublet
caked with black blood. In the market square
threatening murmurs surged.
Soldiers were posted by the stalls to keep order.
From the balconies of the surrounding houses
peered the fat disapproving faces
of middle class mothers, who pointed to the home
of the lovely culprit with its red threshold
and gilded door. They clenched their fists
because justice was too slow. Suddenly the men
took off their hats. Ascending the steps
to the town hall: Lorelei in her veils
and high conical hat, allowing a glimpse
of her red hair sparkling like a goldsmith's work.
It was as though a sudden sun had risen
in the evening shadows.

Lorelei approached, slow and sweet as honey,
her dress was a riot of green arabesques
on a sky-colored ground. No one remembered
the slaughter when they saw her wide blue-green eyes,
the shell-white of her face and her delicate hands.
Hearts beat harder to see her baffled innocence.
The hangman seemed troubled, tears glimmered
in the eyes of the guardsmen who (for all their scars
and beards) were abashed before their task.
The crowd followed close, elbowing each other,
treading heels, till at last they arrived
before the town hall where the merchants came
to pay their taxes, register their holdings,
and have their rights confirmed. The town council stood
without, the entranceway was draped
with cloth of gold, as for a visit from the king.
At the entrance stood an old man, impassive,
though his eyes were red from weeping. The Mayor.
His only son had fallen in the last night's fracas.
Early that morning his wife, a fury,
made him swear to avenge their child
with whom their family name now ended.
And here was the woman who was to blame . . .

"Punish me, my lord," said the guilty girl,
"The earth, it seems, gapes open at my feet,
a chasm into which I am falling, helpless,
taking with me those who love me,
down to death and hell.
Strike me down, strike me dead as my friends
whose bodies still bleed there inside.
I know my doom won't bring them back,
but at least all will see that, without them,
I didn't wish to live. Only remember

I'm just a young woman, too young to bear
long torture. Good my master,
give the order for my death,
but in the name of love, make it rapid."
She crawled imploring towards him,
around her, on the flagstones, trailed her long red hair.

He shook her clasping hands from his knees,
took his seat and asked, "Was anyone here,
noble, bourgeois or peasant, a witness to this crime?
Come forward boldly, describe the deed,
the time, the place. I'm listening."
No response. The elder thought,
"These cursèd stupid people,
these animals, go soft in the head
at the sight of a pretty girl in velvet and pearls."
Thrice he called for witnesses, finally
an old German mercenary emerged
from the crowd, awkward, with distressed expression.

"I tried to intervene in the brawl
for the honor of my calling.
The wine jugs had been emptied, the party was over,
they rolled dice to decide which one would spend the night
with this lady. That started it, with no help from her.
It isn't her fault she looks as she does
and men get jealous. Voices were raised,
someone threw a punch. The slut got scared.
They went to settle things outside.
Ten of them, swords drawn, before her door.
God's blood, what a crash of steel!
Even I felt fear, and the girl was half dead
with terror, screaming 'Murder, help!'
A lot of good that did. Their pages and valets

were upstairs demolishing the leftovers,
licking the plates, not about to drop those
and run to their deaths. She blames herself—
well, if she has admirers she keeps it discreet,
lives quiet, doesn't show herself on the street
except on public holidays. Is she a man-crazy flirt,
like the townsfolk say? So far as I know
she's a game girl, no prim miss,
but she'd never so much as hurt another's feelings.
In the present climate of ill-will towards her
I may as well add my complaint to the rest.
If she really is such a loose woman,
I don't see why she wasn't such with me."
The crowd around Lorelei burst into laughter
and applause at the soldier's tale.

"Traitor!" hissed the mayor between his teeth,
then turning to the woman crouched at his feet,
"Hear that, daughter of shame?"
(He spit the words in her frightened face.)
"This village of idiots absolves you of blame.
Go home. Your crimes aren't in the jurisdiction
of decent people, witch! To atone for your deeds
you ought to walk barefoot to Rome,
there to receive your deserts in a dungeon
or else on an inquisition pyre.
Go, you've groveled long enough
on my floor." With flashing eye he went inside
and left her there alone. The soldiers were dismissed.
She struggled to her feet, with no defense now
against the baffled bloodthirsty crowd
circling round her. Wordless, staring, stupefied,
she heard the cries and curses rise,
threats of damnation, promises of death,
such as people shout when they rise against their masters.

They seized her, dragged her through the square,
the open-air market, street after street,
passed before her as in a dream.
She was carried like a wisp of straw
in an angry flood. She couldn't breathe,
she shut her eyes. Suddenly she stood
before the cathedral's dark portal,
from the choir deep within came the cry of an organ
sonorous, austere, wailing its high crescendo.

Within, a man enthroned by the altar
beneath a velvet canopy. A bishop.
Below him acolytes swung their censers
in slow rhythm. The church was full
from its portals all the way to the gilded screen
at the end of the nave. Beyond it, beneath the apse,
were the choir, the sanctuary, tombs
of the distinguished dead. The crowd, mostly women,
pressed forward to see. In the space before the altar
were trestles erected to receive ten coffins,
darkly draped in funerary finery.

Lorelei was brought to the altar;
behind her, the grieving female mob
all in black. Her red mane hung down,
her teeth nearly chattered with fear, her eyes
were stunned wide, she looked like she was drunk
on the blood shed for her. She gave a cry
that seemed to shake the high stained glass windows,
she fell at the feet of the astonished mitred man,

"Condemn me, father, beat me, I have sinned.
The hidden crime that was my life
has been dragged into daylight. I'm an evil creature,
my kisses have drained the blood of your sons.
Coffins, candles, keening—these are my works.
I tremble at the sight of the cross, I dread
the sound of prayers. I am a vampire.
The people's fear's well placed. Flee me,
I am plague!"

The priest descended in alarm,
the acolytes let their censers dangle
then climbed the seats of the choir to see.
The bishop leaned close to study the face
of the beautiful girl with the red-gold hair.
"She's mad. Where are her parents?"
"Father, she has no family.
This is Lorelei." The priest shuddered
at the name. Never before had he seen her,
this pale courtesan.

"You must find someone else to condemn you to death.
The only sentence I pronounce on you is this:
get you to a nunnery, shave those splendid tresses,
bury that face as dazzling as snow,
those eyes that are enchantments,
in a cloister. Even I can feel their power.
This is the penalty I impose:
on your famous beauty, night;
and silence for your evil fame."
The bishop retreated to his candle-lit
and frankincense shadows, with a troubled look.

II

No sentinels stand guard upon these ramparts,
yellow wall-flowers have overgrown their stones;
the only motion here is when these blooms
are stirred by the breeze.
Here comes a woman, head bowed in shame,
descending the convent's rocky stairs
furtively, as though she sought a place to hide.
Three soldiers follow her, pikes on their shoulders,.
The noon Angelus bell rings out over them.
They're silent, subdued by the August heat.
At times, as they descend the hill,
they get a glimpse of fallow fields
or the Rhine far below. The way is steep
and sun-baked dust white. At times
the woman's cloak parts to show
(like a stream in a summer forest)
the blue and gold of her splendid dress.
The guards catch their breath. Lorelei
is no less Lorelei. The road is rough,
her escort armed, and she is beautiful.
She has no more tears, but looks straight ahead
at the road—wide and frightening as a chasm.
The murderous world, which has no mercy
on innocents, rejects and exiles her.
No pardon, not even justice. All of them—
from the mayor, to that complicit bishop,
to the far-off cloister which opens its gates
even to assassins—all cast her away
with disgust, like rotten fruit. Now Lorelei,
head bowed beneath her shame, rejected by her people,
by the priest with his frigid pity,
she walks, exhausted, beneath the lead-heavy
rays of summer sun.

Where is she going, heart sick with old resentments
and new loathings? To a lepers' hospital,
chosen (with dismal cruelty)
for her future, there to grow old
changing bandages and washing oozy sores.
In the hedges all around her
nesting birds chirp. Poppies blaze
in the fields of ripe wheat. A rising wind
bends the grain, the armed escort,
is a military silhouette
against the azure August sky.
The distant walled town, Lorelei's home,
looks unreal as a stage backdrop,
all slate roofs and slender bell towers,
like a castle bristling with turrets
painted in miniature
on an ancient missal's vellum page.

At the turning of the road she pauses, pale,
unsteady on her feet, as if she were drunk.
She takes in the sky, dazzling as brass,
her town now outlined on the horizon.
Childhood memories return at random:
tender recollections of a poem she'd recited
while plucking a flower's petals one by one;
lost beliefs, angels long since flown.
In rush images of her parents' home,
old and dark, on the outskirts of the noisy crowded town;
her tall frail grandfather with his long white hair,
bent to tend the hearth fire between the gorgon-headed
andirons; her room with hexagonal
leaded windows, their purple stained-glass lilies
made to flame by the dawn,
the pot of basil on the windowsill.

She recalled her first lover,
then the young German soldier, then the captain,
then many a rich and handsome lord
—how proud she'd been—and now? Cursed by all.

Her eyes, dull and fixed
like those of someone who's been tortured,
turned to her escorts impatient of more delay.
Calmly she unfastened her heavy necklace
(with its great aquamarine, a goldsmith's masterpiece)
from her splendid neck. She said, "Let this repay you
for the time it takes for one last look
at my home, a last goodbye, the final wish
of an exile. Let me stand on this cliff
that overlooks the river, fix in memory
my country, my childhood, all I leave.
Indulge a poor madwoman. You smile?
Yes, it's foolish, but the foolish hearts of women
live and die for such." As she spoke, her look
became soft, endearing, irresistible
as it had been when she'd commanded dukes
and barons. He beauty seemed royal,
holy, intoxicating! All together they said yes,
as though they'd been that lady's squires.

She stood then on that rocky prominence,
smiling at her captors, exalted, glorious,
shining like a pearl against the velvet reds
of sunset, her hair transfigured in its rays.
"I forgive you, guilty, stupid world,
and entrust myself to you, last refuge
of the wretched, old Father Rhine."
She crossed her arms

over her bosom, closed her eyes.
As if in a dream, she fell forward.

While the river carried away the body
of the beautiful criminal, the three armed men
crouched on the rock and argued
about how much they could get for the necklace.

THE PERFUME OF ANTIQUITY

THE GOLDEN CUP

for Madame Judith Gautier[16]

A dying king once let fall a golden cup
into the sea's blue abyss;
that chalice was the symbol of his soul's enigma.
The waves sang, in hoarse choir,
the sad ballad of his life.

He shivered in the cold north wind,
propped himself against the balustrade,
let the cup slip from his fingers
like fruit so ripe it falls by itself,
like a pearl returned to the deeps whence it came,
like a tear yielded to the meaningless brine.

Leaning out over ocean's infinity,
he had kissed with trembling lip the rim
of the cup that had held his happiness.
The sea intoned its unending wordless dirge,
blood thundered love's tocsin in his ears.

Like him, I lost the gold cup
my hands could not hold.
Since then, how many a glass have I held
from which I tried in vain to drink oblivion?

A GOLDEN DREAM IT WAS

for Madame Judith Gautier

A golden dream it was; to the music of the surf
we walked along the shore, forgetful of self,
gazing into the distance, all the world effaced
from our souls by the waves. You leaned on me
as we walked, arm in arm.

A golden dream it was, the ocean left long
complicated tresses of seaweed outstretched
along the beach, wreathes and twisted ribbons
of vegetable jade, unholy foliage
from the gardens of the drowned.

A golden dream it was. The ocean played and sprayed,
rolled its evanescent lacework of foam,
white as the gulls that strutted on the sand.

The halcyon was a mythical bird
the ancients believed could charm winter waves
to calm, so it could brood in its floating nest—

your love was just such an impossible halcyon,
a wingèd dream lost to the fog,
passed beyond my horizon,
leaving to me barren shore
and the unintelligible sound of the sea.

WHEN I WAS A CHILD [17]

for my mother

When I was a child I wandered through the fields
and the old church rang its distant Angelus,
the sun-glimmered stream, the breeze-borne bee,
whispered only for me.

The stained-glass saints with their long gray beards
in the high choir windows joined their hands
to pray a blessing on my curly head.

Down country roads where wild cherries darkened
into sweetness, cornflowers peered
after me in their splendid blue ruffs.

Did I make you cry? The day, dispelling mist
gemmed with dew the flowers that it opened.

A dream! The dawn of love,
announced by the lilies' soundless trumpets,
the wide skies of my childhood.

FLORENCE

for Madame la Comtesse de Bonis[18]

I

What music there is in your very name, O Florence!
An echo of the poetry, the battles, the banquets
of medieval Italy.

Where are they now, the scholars and musicians,
proud rulers of cities, writers, lunatics,
the women who still look back at us,
immortal, from their portraits,
whose courtly lovers knelt to kiss
the hems of their dresses?

Where is it now, that world whose glory and madness
intoxicates us yet? Once your whims, O Florence,
were Italy's laws, when you set a Medici
on Peter's throne to build that great basilica:
Leo the Tenth, who thought he could drown out
the shouts of Luther with the exquisite singing
of the papal choir;

when Rome was once again the center of the world,
when Dante, Petrarch, Machiavelli
and Michelangelo walked through Florence
where the Medici erected a palace
so much more than royal.

II

Abandoned the palace, silent the bells
in their slender towers, these long stifling nights
of August. The moon turns the emptiness
into a silent silvery dream.

Were Dante to wander here one midnight,
led by Virgil to the Limbo
that had been his Florence,
he'd stand there sadly on the Arno's shore,

he'd stare at the marble stairs
of the De Bonis mansion, gleaming in the dark.
Seeing it deserted, he'd say,

"Old Florence is finally gone,
there'll never be another Beatrice here."

APOLLONIA

for Madame la Marquise d'Hèricourt[19]

Hail to you, Apollonia! In defiance of two
Christian millennia, you've a pagan name.
The old Greek syllables
still shape a living word
from the language once spoken by Euripides.

A word, a recollection
—sad as acanthus leaves
on a broken temple frieze
that once stood white against an azure Attic sky.

Hail to the genius of the Greeks! Hail to you
whose beauty is ever new!
You would have made the young men of Sparta
tremble like the flowers that bloom in its ruins.

A LORD'S PRIVILEGE[20]

The lord was handsome, young, with a dark complexion,
and a liking for the ladies. The bride was twenty,
in a dress that expressed as much as it concealed
her charms. He veil was fine lace, she wore
the high conical hat with silver trim
of a medieval lady. He white linen purse
was embroidered, like her dress, in matte gold.
With a pretty face, a winning expression,
sweet and modest, gleaming hair tied back,
delicate hands, large blue eyes,
snowy bosom, scarlet smiling lips,
rosy and appealing, she was a morsel
worthy of a lord.

The lord in question
looked quite romantic too, tall and dark.
He'd already caught her hands (which she'd tried to hide
in her lace cuffs). Now they walked together, arm in arm,
he held her hand in his, leaned in, talking low,
smiling. Guillemette, the bride—
she really can't refuse. But in front of all these people?
"Oh count, the entire village is watching,
you put me to the blush! Wait until later . . ."

"—No one will notice. Along those stairs
no one goes but pages, armed retainers, squires

and servants carrying smoking silver platters
of roasted chicken, pheasants served in their feathers.
Right here there's no one but fat veterans
at table, daggers in their belts, drinking deep,
slovenly untucked shirts hanging out
of their unbuttoned doublets."

In the courtyard, along the road,
the rabble eat and drink, stretched out on the ground.
They enjoy themselves chatting, laughing at each other's
questionable jokes. Guillemette, inside
with just the lord and his servants now,
as though she were herself a great lady.
He calls her *ma chère*, and says such things
as make her tremble and redden
right down to her bosom. "To be sure, your lordship's
a very great lord, but even a serf
has the right to self-respect."

She's offended, pushes him away,
but how can you be angry with this elegant fellow
when his beard feels so silky against your cheek,
when his aristocratic long-fingered hands
so shimmer with rings? Especially when your husband's
ugly and dull. She doesn't think or see
too clearly now, the wine's gone to her head.
The eyes of the count are velvet-soft
and fire-warm. He whispers to her,
they walk along the torchlit hallway
—and so, goodnight husband!

The manor door shuts with a quiet but decided
thud. The halberds of the doormen
glitter under the stars. Here's the new groom

nervously turning his new velvet hat
with its handsome ribbon round and round
in his hands. Beside the befooled newlywed,
a fat Flemish monk in vestments points to heaven,
with a grave imposing air, invites the man
to submit himself to the deity's will,

"The soul belongs to God, but the body to one's lord."

SUNT LACRIMAE RERUM[21]

Even nature has its griefs, its tears.
Let English gardens offer an eternal springtime,
a riot of roses, gladiolas opening
their petals as if to laugh,
uninhibited, stamens and pistils in the wind!

A garden from the days of Louis the Fifteenth,
behind the metal grate of its ancient gate,
with crumbling benches, neglected fishpond,
in which the trees, planted in a geometric patterns,
are reflected sadly and seem sadly to reflect—
such gardens have their own autumnal charm.

One senses here the perfume of another age,
(notes of clove, orris, orange-flowers, sandalwood),
like a sweet spectral presence. A teasing breeze
recalls the ladies' fans of that long dead century
until dusk muffles the scene into dream.

THE HIGHWAY[22]

for my mother

Evening, morning, I sit at my window,
resting my chin in my palms,
watching the highway that hugs the hills
till it disappears in the distance.

When the setting sun is an ember-red blur
in the misty sky of a cloudy day,
I sit and watch, as if in a dream,
that highway climbing the cliffs.

The road unrolls its distant ribbon,
snaking away—to where?
It leaves behind this stupid mean town.
Does it lead to happiness? To exile?

The rise of the road invites me to go,
promises better beyond the horizon,
offers the utter freedom of clouds.
The open road's the terrestrial
echo of the boundless heavens.

Does it lead to a land of love and rosebuds?
To flowering lilies, to a bluer sky?
To a world your tearful eyes now seek and see
only in your dreams?

A loveless home, a passionless life,
in-laws you only baffle,
here the scent of the blossoming orange grove
seems sweet and unreal as happiness.

But one becomes comfortable. One becomes numb.
One says, "Not today,"
and sits at the window to stare at the road.

One day you can't wait any longer,
you get up to go—but your own last sad
backward glance stops you at the threshold.

The cliffs in the distance have disappeared,
fog hides the highway, the horizon's lost
along with your dreams. It's too late to leave.

FORGOTTEN

for Madame Heuzé[23]

Forgetting, the final mercy
mankind takes on history—
it doesn't apply on the personal scale.
There, old griefs abide,
choke hope.

Bitter rememberings
eat into the heart,
like red rust
rotting through metal.

Useless treasure, our tears,
like a rare perfume
kept in a vial of bright
unforgiving crystal.

We all cherish in memory
some failed dream, of love or success,
closed carefully in its coffin,

an undead presence
no one would suspect,
which keeps us from sleep.

HORIZON

for Madame la Marquise d'Héricourt

Looking out to sea at dawn—what do they mean
these dark amber waves,
these rainbow-colored clouds
on the horizon, as the sun makes its eternal return,
seemingly ideal,
like on the first of all dawns
when the stars all sang together
and the angels shouted for joy?

A pale day returns to we who stand upon these sands.
Monotonous, the sound of the surf,
the gray of the waves!
On the horizon the sun is dawning over ocean.
Are they out there somewhere, beyond these seas,
our true native shores? Are we merely exiles here?

The sea wind, the roarings of the waters, rise,
insistent, unintelligible,
like the sound of someone shouting
in the distance—you can't make out the words.

O sky, you who are the shore's blue dream,
O surf, you that seem to give voice to our longings,
O horizon, glimmering vision that reveals
that the ocean is the very sister of our soul.

HAROLD[24]

for Alfred Lord Tennyson

I

That's where she lives, beyond the foggy horizon,
daughter of the dark North Sea's agèd king.
She rules a little island in the amethystine blue
where white seabirds rest on their furthest flights.

They rest there, leaving down and moulted feathers
in frost-colored eddies on the sand.
Foam-bordered waves, ruddy in the dawn light,
are all that covers the princess
swimming naked in the surge.

Sunrise wakes her, moonlight soothes her,
her clothes are seaweed green, her comb's the gold
of sunken treasure, in the current the curls
of her honey-colored hair, honey-slow, unfurl.

She sings by starlight, naked, playing her harp.
She laughs to see the sails of Norman pirates
far off, white, flying before the wind.

II
Harold's Song

"On a wondrous stormy day, when the wind from the wings
of a tempest churns the sea milk-white and hides the reefs,
when even seagulls fight for life,
struggling to make shore,
with nearly human cries;

"hippocamps, sea-monsters, half-horse, half-fish,
whipped on by the wind, rear up, water pouring
off them in liquid silver, hooves tearing
at the air. I leap on the back of the foremost,
hold onto its mane
and rebellious neck.

"I spur you on with the butt of my spear,
O fierce Hippocamp! I,
the exiled archangel,
son of the bitter abyss!

"We fly through the waves, my mount dishevels the sea,
wild with rage and despair.
There ahead is the North Sea's daughter on her isle."

III

Knees clamped to the scaly monster's flanks,
he himself scaled and shiny as a fish
in his silver armor, blond Harold charges,
singing as he does when he goes into battle.

The beaten hippocamp now tamely obeys.
Harold's horn announces his wedding day
as he storms the sea king's blue castle.

The princess strokes the muzzle of the hippocamp,
smiling, naked in the waves, she seems
like a lily in a pale blue stream.
The sky turns wintry gray,

and already the waters have closed over them both,
devouring the dream. The flood of the real
dissolving, as it always does, the ideal.

THE DEEP

for Jean Richepin[25]

I

Unheard-of poems, legends of ancient worlds
sunk to crumble beneath the green waves,
pearls that gleam unseen on ocean floor,
dreams of the deep, the fierce old voice of sea—

such are your songs, Richepin, they laugh
like a flock of bright-eyed sea nymphs playing in the waves
by the blond sandy shore—or else they resound
like the melancholy echoing waves that break
against the cliffs, implacably sad
as the sinking of centuries into bygone time.

The sea is not without its history, its kings:
the crowns of the drowned yet glimmer
in the undulant enchantment of seaweed groves below,

the lost palace of Ys, king of Cornwall,
its watery halls now visited by fish;
the undersea demons Solomon controlled
with his magic ring, the sunken unsunned
wonders of fishermen's dreams.

II

The soul, no less than the ocean,
is an infinite thing. On the surface all may glitter
but within is hidden a shadowed vastness
where lost worlds turn in their uncanny sleep.

Disappointed hopes, a race of dreams,
circulate still in those strong undercurrents
through the gardens of the drowned.
At times they rise
to darken even the brightest eyes,

and sometimes a ray of light penetrates
this abyss of ancient pain and sleeping griefs,
then a treasure gleams golden in the green deep,

then the scornful cynic with his cold clear laugh
feels his heart,
which he'd thought dead to feeling such as this,
beat with sweet and urgent heat.

THREE POEMS FOR SULLY PRUDHOMME[26]

I

Why struggle to fan life back into embers
when the ashes and the hearthstone are cold?

There never can be tears enough
to revive the reeds that once grew
on the banks of a stream long since run dry.

You found me still bleeding from another love,
her sunset's red seemed to be your dawn.

I loved, if not you, your generous error,
you were thoughtful as a sister,
and, like a mother, kind.

Yes, selfishly I let you give me your heart,
trusting to your sympathy
that you'd forgive my deceit.

I wasn't toying with you,
didn't mean to cheat you,
I was sick and you had the power to heal.

Your touch soothed my wound.
How could I tell you I didn't love you back?
How could I return hurt for your smiles?
How could I reject what you so gladly gave?

I was miserable. I asked much of you.
I wanted everything—but love.

Greedily I accepted your pity,
like a starving dog
that wants to be petted and fed.
Not even a dog—for I didn't repay
your care with loyalty and love.

Though I've failed to show you gratitude
at least I can offer honesty.
Give me now the contempt
my cowardice deserves.

II
Caprice

Dear soul, if only we had met
a year ago, I would have seen
in you a dream made real—
I would have fallen in love with you.

But, had I felt that passion,
would you have loved me in return?
I doubt it. We flee whoever wants us,
we're drawn to cold, not heat.

My boredom, my indifference,
as boundless as a desert's sands,
validated me for you,
dazzled you like a winter's day.

My scorn was lofty, alluring
like the snow of a frozen peak
no sun will melt, to which no steps
can ever ascend.

You drank the waters of a mirage,
that glittering fiction made you drunk.

Take comfort though, not you alone,
but everyone believes most deeply
only in the impossible.

III
The Rendez-Vous

Do you remember yet, madame,
our farewells on that final day
on the gloomy shore? It was just us,
the season for the beach was past,
we walked alone.

Early October it was, the sea
was a vivid, even garish, blue.
The rocky cliffs in the distance
were stark and black.

We sat at the base of the crags
dreamily reliving the summer

with the unspoken sorrow of those
who know they'll never meet again.

We both know now how matters stood.
I knew you suffered, loving me,
and I—was merely kind, my care
was nothing more than brotherly.

You looked so very charming then!
I still recall the way you drew
your shawl more close against the cold,
the weariness in your eyes.

With your ample lace neck-cloth
and your earrings of pendant pearls,
you looked like a girlish page-boy
from the court of a Valois king.

I looked at you with an ardor
I couldn't hide—your voice, your look,
reminded me precisely
of a woman I'd loved long ago.

I sat with her, as now with you,
upon this shore. In your blue eyes
I saw her gaze, which answered mine then
with an exquisite irony.

Her mocking glance, coolly amused
by my love, her rich, thick hair
which it nearly made me drunk
just to see.

It all came back, how much it meant
to me, those first avowals of love,
her tearful eyes, how strangely
she laughed, as if at herself.

After a month I saw her again,
riding back from the forest
with the duke—her exaggerated surprise
at seeing me, as though she barely
remembered who I was.

The icy politeness of her lackeys
in their stiff embroidered livery,
the scorn with which they told me
when I called, "Madame has gone out."

I lived it all again, the snubs,
the rage I couldn't show,
my cowardice—it all came back,
I felt my face burn.

A flood of feeling, unexpressed,
was overwhelming me within.
I felt like a drunk exposed
to the disapproving looks of passers-by.

Old anger returned, the ancient wound
re-opened. I cursed you in my heart,
you, innocent. You couldn't know
how much I wanted to hurt you.

But you sensed something. You rose
with a distracted air, you said,
"We really ought to go."
Reluctantly I followed.

We walked back up the beach,
each of us staring at the rainy horizon,
each in our own dream.

I looked with dull despairing eye
at the catastrophe of waves
against the rocks beneath the gray
autumnal sky.

You, calmer but more sad,
felt pity for the early frost
that had settled on my selfish heart,
deadening its early spring
before it had really felt anything.

IN THE WOMEN'S QUARTERS

for my friend Jean Gounod[27]

Before a full-length Venetian mirror,
in a great chair brocaded with coats of arms,
sits a young boy. Behind him, their bare arms
weighted with precious heavy bracelets,
wearing ruby necklaces that shine like spilt blood
against their white necks, stand Isaure and Paula
in long splendid dresses. The room is high-ceilinged,
paneled in black wood, the parqueted floor gleams
like a mirror. The walls' cornices and panels
are carved with saints and heraldry.
The curtains and upholstery are an orgy
of colors. At the far end of the room,
like a precious conflagration,
a stained-glass window shows dwarves blowing horns.

The boy is delicate, golden-haired, slender,
elegant in his movements
as a thoroughbred greyhound.
Trustful, he sprawls in the chair
like the touching subject of a sentimental painting,
a Boucher Cupid. His long hair has been braided,
his shirt is half-unbuttoned.
The two girls stand laughing,
deciding what he'll wear.

To look at their sparkling eyes and smiles,
their hesitant gestures, their shy undecided
boldness, their nervous daring hilarity,
their indoor pallor, their eyes of velvet and fire,
the dark heavy manes of their hair—
all declare that this palace is their cloister.
The debilitating life of the women's quarters
is killing them. Desire, too successfully repressed,
has driven them to deliberately, obsessively
strip the boy.

There's a priest who guards
this harem which only the king's allowed to enter;
the girls keep their fingers busy with needlework
while they dream of passion and tournament knights.

Ah the burning, the yearning, the boredom of hours
bent over embroidery, the hot summer nights
when even a light shift feels oppressive,
not to mention the dull endless winter days.
Then the joyous cries when the agèd priest
leads in their prepubescent cousin
Jehan (Lord of Este and of Côme)
who visits them once every month or so.

They'd heard his horse's hooves on the cobbles
below the palace balcony. Young Jehan
was really too pretty to be a boy,
so they dressed the little gentleman
up as a girl. He's been there since very early,
so you can imagine what kisses, what liberties
those two have already permitted themselves,
the sweet games, giggles, secrets, whispered admissions,
raids on the candy dishes, looking at pictures

set like jewels in the pages of rich missals,
toys taken up and cast aside.
They danced as they sang catches from ballads
and troubador songs. They teased their old dog
who finally retreated, sulking, to the room's
far corner where it dozes on a cushion now.
They finally decided that the best fun of all
would be to dress their dear cousin up
in girl's clothes. At first he blushed,
didn't want (or dare?) to. They'd made up their minds.
At last he gave up warding them off,
let his arms fall.

It was an uncanny whim!
They had him step into a scarlet dress.
How odd it was to see his thin boy's body
swimming in brocade. They powdered his face,
framed it in a lady's cap of fine lace.
He looked like an antique formal portrait
of the Flemish school. The girls crowed with triumph.
It was all too perfect, those lovely shoulders,
those fine white arms! Conspiratorial
looks and kisses were exchanged.
Then down to the serious business of deciding
Jehan's new name. Odette or Nancy?
Isaure favors Nancy, Paula prefers Odette.
It seemed the debate might take a serious turn,
will against will, as in a joust
when both opponents thunder forward
with lances leveled. Combat must decide
the right. The fatal struggle was interrupted
when a pearl bracelet Jehan had been fiddling with
broke. The silver-gray spheres scattered
with a clatter across the polished floor.
Laughter ended the battle.

Jehan, like a loyal squire, scrambled
to gather the precious runaways. These he poured
into Paula's cupped hands, kissing her fingertips
submissively. The three of them
looked like a nest of turtledoves,
you wouldn't have been surprised to see
real wings on the backs of these three
wee angels.

The setting sun shone directly
through the stained glass window, bathing them all
in red splendor. In that magic light
the tall girls laughing with that feminine imp
trapped between them—you'd think you'd come upon
two elven maidens giving a bath
to a captive reluctant blond goblin.

Charming! But every day ends.
The sun is setting. The gothic window darkens.
Their elder sister, Mahaut, prettiest
of the three, stands on the balcony
of her room, staring into space.
Beside her the priest, a discreet and eloquent man,
observes with approval her eyes fixed on heaven,
and a flock of cranes, in triangle formation,
crosses the evening sky.

FOR MADAME LACROIX[28]

I can see you as a maiden in ancient Greece,
tall, athletic, splendid,
a quiver on your back, a bow in your hand,
a golden band cinching your tunic
high up, giving an interesting
emphasis to your small boyish bosom.
Your skirt falls only to mid-thigh,
allowing your legs the freedom a huntress needs,
while showing to advantage your long and shapely legs.
—you seem like a classical statue come
abruptly to life—alarmingly divine.

I can see you striding in high-strapped sandals,
a Diana, a bacchante. Standing, you might be
a caryatid, a living pillar,
towering over me, marble-pink and perfect.

A goddess with a halo of moonbeams;
a priestess of Bacchus crowned with ivy,
a fierce proud daughter of the forest
or a templed deity.

ANDREA FOSCARI

for Armand Silvestre[29]

Andrea Foscari, the Cardinal of Ragusa's
little minion, had the fresh pink lips
of a pretty child. His dagger was a triumph
of the goldsmith's art, his delicate fingers
were weighted with exquisite rings.

His horse was shod with silver, the jewels
and precious metal thread of his embroidered cloak:
a flowered ground on which was emblazoned
his family arms.

Bathed in a rainbow of stained-glass light,
he traced the cardinal's lips
with a single finger
and asked, in the wheedling tones of a royal boy
who wants a new weapon or gem,
for the deaths of Parma's king and Ferrara's duke.

RENAISSANCE

for Armand Silvestre

Hail to thee, O Renaissance, enchanted forest
where Diana de Poitiers, mistress of the king,
was a goddess. In the mirror of art
we see her still, bathing like her namesake
in a woodland pool, half-hidden by reeds,
listening to distant hunting horns,
admiring her naked reflection.

Leaning against a tame stag, she smiles,
her marble limbs are dazzling silvery white.
Her tall hunting bow and the towering antlers
of the stag curve together above her,
like the branches of winter trees.

A slender greyhound licks her ivory foot,
which Eros himself might have sculpted;
she displays herself, white and icy,
naked and unashamed as a lily.

Her tiny breasts, her high diadem,
her snowy shoulders evoke an age of female power
when she made a king young enough to be her son
her pet, and ruled from the Louvre.

TO A GENIUS[30]

I

Sweet, powerful artist, laurel-crowned,
you walk forward carrying a wondrous bouquet
of lilies—white as the dawn of art
that filled your heart—lilies you gathered
from books and dreams.

Faith (who is an exile nowadays),
she's yet beside you, smiling;
Love (who's lost, perhaps damned, among us)
gives you a final kiss as you lie on your bier.
Faith and Love remain immortal, for their names resound
in your sad and touching poems.

You were Faust in the garden of Marguerite,
where the darkness was transfigured by hidden love;
yours was the farewell to Juliette
standing on her balcony, in the hour when larks
start their song. You were Romeo
when he wed her in the grave.

Blessèd art thou, O poet,
singer of Love's requiem;
the lilies of art and feeling
reopened at your touch,
and at yours alone.

II

We will go together, carrying palm-branches
(the ancient world's emblem of victory)
for you, for as long as the heavens of art
are bright, we, the child Tomorrow,
and old man Yesterday.

We'll follow where you've led, drunk with suffering,
yet glad to have felt so much,
and raise to your creations a marble monument
by the shore, beneath Italian skies.

A cortège of archangels in dazzling robes
will surround you, playing lutes. A shower of petals
will fall from the heavens to mark your apotheosis,
you who sang with such happy passion
the vanished classical world.

THE SWANS

for a departed lady

There's a doleful poem that Tennyson wrote
about an old king, whose beard was white
as sea-foam, how he stood on the shore below his castle
sadly watching the sunset. [31]

He saw a flock of swans
fly across the darkening sky
like fugitive hopes.

You passed across my heavens like those swans,
a vision brief and rare
as a dream of happiness.

THE BLOOD OF THE GODS

EPHEBES

for Gustave Flaubert[32]

Risen from the long-dead centuries
like a strangely troubling perfume,
these phantom beings—like slender, naked
archangels; without clothing, without names,
without a gender, dancing before the shrines
of less expected gods.

Creatures of filth and splendor,
lips shaped for forbidden kisses,
beings of the sewer as much as of the temple—
you despise them? They retaliate
with demons' triumphant laughter!

Sculpted on Grecian pediments
(like the frontispiece of an erotic book),
I have sketched them in these pages,
crowned their brows with lilies;
for me, these creatures have their own eternity.

Beautiful, stupid, tragic
figures in the antique style,
boys, but in subtle, disquieting ways
more feminine than girls.

GANYMEDE[33]

Young Ganymede stands beside the throne of Zeus,
mortal boy in the glory of an eternal world,
sweet, serious, the servant of a deity's desires,
the pleasure of which suffuses his face
with a drunken flush.

Ganymede's hair is wavy and dark,
like a sea you wouldn't trust your boat to.
His narrow brow, his big wondering eyes,
have the solemn dreamy stupidity
that befits the passive lover
of a perverted god.

Reluctant but resigned accomplice
of Jupiter's erotic misdeeds;
no matter how monstrous, this child only smiles
or brays with pagan laughter,
moronic and insolent.

He lifts the amphora to pour, he tilts it,
slowly, carefully, intent upon his service,
he fills the dazzling chalice
with nectar and offers it blushing
to the decadent Caesar of Olympus.

SHEPHERD BOY ALEXIS

All alone in the depths of an ancient wood,
shepherd boy Alexis couldn't have been more handsome
if his father had been a god. He listens
to the sounds of the forest, echoes them in music,
fingers nimble on the openings of his flute.

Age seventeen, he roves at dawn;
his full lips were made for wild berries,
and his thick red hair to glow golden in the sun.

He's strong, masculine, but his chin hasn't yet
any need of a razor. Fauns, who spy on him,
entranced by his adolescent beauty,
don't dare risk his indignant glance.

Alexis is chaste. The other shepherds make him presents
of nuts and fruit. Their woodland gifts
are wasted. No one has touched,
much less plucked, this virgin wildflower.

NARCISSUS

Beside a clear pond on a bank all starry
with asphodels, the handsome shepherd boy
Narcissus, whose very name makes goddesses
(and certain gods) dream—Narcissus
lies here on his stomach, eyes half-closed,
sprawled like one exhausted from love.

He lets his head hang over the water
as if it were too heavy for his slender neck;
he gazes, dazed, at his own reflection.
In his eyes there's a beautiful stupidity,
his lovely slack mouth gapes, he sighs,

"I love you. I love you. Why can't I touch you,
my sweet, my second Narcissus?" The effort
of his longing makes his smooth adolescent forehead
sparkle with perspiration. He stretches
closer to the mirrory pool.

He shudders, swoons with a private pleasure
that can never be enough, then, drained by passion,
he lies as if dead among the waterside irises.

HYLAS[34]

In the shady deep woods, Hylas, his amphora
on his shoulder, is a proud, serious-looking youth.
He bends down among the reeds
to fill his vessel from the stream,
with a gentle half-smile, intent upon his work.

Beneath his high noble brow, his eyes
are bluer than the sky. He's naked
except for a loin-cloth. The rays of sunset
bathe his pallor with a ruddy blush
as if to emphasize how ripe he is for love.

His golden curls are tawny
in the twilight's last gleaming. Hercules himself
has kissed those shoulders, white and splendid
as lilies against the forest green.

He daydreams,
never dreaming that this spring is enchanted.
He's thrilled to hear his own name vaguely
uttered in the rippling silver voice of the stream . . .

YOUNG BACCHUS

Bacchus, god of the golden world
of those who are drunk—what irony there is
in the near-sneer of his delicious lips.
His eyes, beneath his sleepy half-closed lids
miss nothing. His golden skin is pale,
as the gleam of gold, or like the white bloom
on ripe golden grapes.

He rides his chariot in triumph, through deep woods,
it's drawn by a team of panthers; he's nude,
as is the way with gods. A troop of naked maidens
precede the deity, dancing, brandishing
shields and swords.

Female lions rove the hillsides, enraged
by something other than hunger.
Their great throats utter the low guttural thunder
of a great cat's roar. Bacchus laughs his approval.
The god who is wine (the solvent of shame)
savors love in all its non-ordinary forms.

BATHYLLUS[35]

In the depths of a back-alley tavern
frequented only by sailors,
Bathyllus, the handsome Thracian,
slender and feminine,
dances to the music of flutes and tambourines,
bracelets of bells clash on his ankles
in time, he plucks the petals from a rose
as he steps, and lets his tunic part—

it opens like a flower, disclosing
his flat bosom, nipples enlarged with rouge,
a subtly muscled dancer's belly,
the dark curling hair that frames his pink
and perfect flower.

The music stops. Bathyllus freezes
in a hieratic pose. With a look
that doesn't seem quite human,
he transfixes the sailors who watch with open
mouths and wider eyes.
He offers to their doglike adoring kisses
the palms of his perfumed hands.

ATTIS[36]

Attis, distracted, flees the goddess' temple
in his blue woman's tunic broidered with golden stars.
He wanders past the water-lily pond,
reeds brush his hairless legs.

His long black hair is artfully braided,
bracelets shaped like serpents encircle his forearms,
his lips are painted, his eyes enlarged with kohl,

he stands by the fountain that feeds the lotus pool,
opens his robe, surveys with disdain
his still half-masculine torso.

"My nipples will never bud
on larger, darker areolas,
my breasts will never swell. Didn't I deserve
better than his flat chest
after I bled between my legs
in such cruel puberty?"

PATROCLUS[37]

In Achilles' tent, beside his armor,
lies beautiful Patroclus, once the pride
of Thrace's flowery meadows, where he hunted,
outpacing the deer in his splendid blue-dyed sandals,
their golden buckles inset with red gems.

Patroclus is pallid, his eyes forever closed;
Achilles' long blond hair unbound
falls about his face. He holds the hero's
feet in his hands and kisses them.

"Nevermore will these run to meet me,
nevermore will those arms embrace me;
your eyes, your violet eyes, will never
look on me again."

Achilles remembers through his painful rage
how often they fought, undefeated, side by side—
Achilles lies beside the beloved cadaver
wishing he too might die.

ANTINOUS[38]

The Nile's cold waters still remember you, O youth,
as do your brothers so many centuries later—
they see you in their dreams, crowned with lotus,
they adore your pornographic immortality.

For a decade Rome knelt to kiss your feet,
those ivory feet that moved a Caesar to tears.
You stand there, splendid, on the threshold
of the Christian centuries, smiling
your scorn for their disapproval.

Your lovely feet, adorned with ankle bracelets
and toe rings—Hadrian pressed his lips to them,
stiff and cold on the imperial bier,

royal boy! He had you sculpted as Bacchus,
Osiris, Apollo, perfectly naked
and nakedly perfect, as only deity can be.

You preside, millennia after your death,
in the eternal Rome of decadent sex.

PRINCESS AUDOVERE[39]

In the silent woods, not far from the cloister
where Frankish kings sleep in their splendid tombs,
see, the princess Audovere,
with her long golden hair and pensive look.

Her skin looks particularly pearl-white
here in the holy gloom of the forest.
Unsmiling, she walks slowly, dreaming
her proud and secret dreams,
this motherless princess.

Her dress is bordered with large embroidered clover,
she strolls beneath the giant oaks
by streams where the wild mint grows.
Her dress trails over the tortured roots
of those enormous trees, and their leaves
shimmer, more vividly green.

In the centuried grove of this cloister park
she passes her days, awaiting the return
of a king in his sixties, her father,
eagerly as if he were her young fiancé.

She walks along the primrose hedge,
drunk with the thought of his victories.
How gladly she imagines the battle,
all those princes slain . . .

She gathers scarlet foxglove flowers
and lilies, white with golden pistils.
He lips part with cruel pleasure
as she pictures butchered kings,
their dead faces pale as these lilies,
their blood red as foxglove.
She holds her bouquet to her nose, inhales,
then, with slow obsessive pleasure,
plucks them, petal by petal, apart.

Fields of battle, bloodstained meadows
where dying princes groan their last
pinioned beneath their fallen horses—
such things please proud maidens.

Mothers have a horror of blood,
they tremble to think, "Is my darling boy safe?"
Virgins see things differently,
they've never suffered, they've never truly wept,
they don't know what it is to give birth,
they really don't care.

Audovere, in the shade of giant trees
smiles to think of the handsome dead,
their long blond hair matted with blood,
fallen like flowers in the red meadow
how she'd daintily step over them
lifting the clover-patterned hem of her dress.

The woods are calm, the cloister severe
in its beauty, deeply sleep the kings
in their sacred tombs. She sleeps too,
the golden-haired princess.

She dreams, with a stern little grin,
she dreams of things no one would guess,
this princess perfect as a pearl,
so lovely, so lonely, so cruel.

ENNOIA[40]

Chilperic, the Frankish king, controlled northern France
and had ambitions for north-west Germany.
He was heading home one evening, gloomy and exhausted,
his men were heavy laden with golden crosses,
enameled silver ciboria and suchlike treasures
looted from rich abbeys on land his brothers owned.
He saw, crouching at the side of the road,
barefoot, her chin on her knees, with red mane,
a motionless maiden. She seemed to be asleep.

Standing watch beside her, was an old bald man
dressed in the rough apparel of a peasant.
The sun, from a pitilessly pure
blue and cloudless sky, made the woman's hair
glow like iron heated in a fire.
The wheat fields around them shone golden
in the brightness.

There was something uncanny about her,
this still woman whose tawny locks blazed.
Chilperic reined his horse. At his signal
the lords and retainers who followed him halted
with a crash of armor and loot. He made a sign
to the woman to rise and approach him.

She only knelt, he face half hid
behind her hands and the hair that hung to her waist.
She didn't see him or hear his troop.
The old man turned to the king whose face
was already pale with impatient rage.
With a palsied tremor of his head, he said,

"She's in a trance."
The king saw then that before this rag-clad
woman was a brass bowl in which a strange light
danced like fire, but it was not flame.
Like a will 'o the wisp, it flickered weird and pale
as a captive soul. Chilperic's men
were ready to head away, they were scared,
so was Chilperic, still, he had to find out
who she was. He gaped as he watched
the man set aside the basin with its flame
and help her up. Her thin face didn't lack
a certain sweetness beneath the grime.
Her arms were nicely shaped, though bruised;
had she hurt herself in some convulsion?
Her hair had captured several nettles,
her eyes were dull, saw nothing, even so
she had a certain solemnity. The king
leaned forward in his saddle to look,
and couldn't look at her enough.

"She's an orphan, sire. I pitied her.
She's followed me now for many a year.
We wander and beg together." "She's dumb?"
"Yes—well, no—sometimes she goes a year
without speaking, then she regains her senses
and says astounding things for days on end.
Folk follow us then, to hear her oracles."

"Make her say something," said Chilperic
with a look admitting of no demur.
The man said, "Speak, Ennoia,
tell us your dreams."

Then, slowly, in a voice as eerie
as night wind whining along the shore,
she spoke. The voice didn't seem to be hers,
it sounded so far away, so sad,
like a doleful echo, a memory
of ancient pain. The child said,

"Eden, dear lying paradise,
with that tremendous tree. After dark its fruit
glowed like gentle round lanterns. Tigers
and wolves slept tamely together in its roots.
Angels perched among its branches;
when they flew off, they left a streak of light
behind them fading slowly to the night.
I listened, enchanted, to the voice of one invisible
who gave me secret sweet advice.
My ears were drunk with its peculiar music.
That golden voice! In the perfumed forest,
so dense it muffled all other sound,
I drank in his powerful, romantic words
which thrilled my pounding heart."

"But, that's Eve!"
cried the Frankish king.

"Don't disturb her dream
or the spirit will fall silent," said the man
and raised two fingers to his lips.

She continued to dolefully intone.

"Our sail bellied out, our galley cut the waves,
hurling foam. I smiled for him, looking
into his eyes, in dread lest I displease him,
and he said to me. 'What do I care
for the grudging favor of the gods?
What's it to me, whether there's peace
between my people and the Greeks?
You'll live in my palace, you will be mine.'

"It was a sweet existence. A tower room,
an ivory bed spread with panther skins,
the way he knelt at my feet
on the thick rich Turkish rugs.
The war forgotten, inaudibly far off,
and he spent the days telling me stories
and stroking my hair.

"At night we would climb to the parapet,
exhausted and dreamy from making love,
we'd peer through the crenels
between the massy merlons
at the Greek camp's sentries and watchfires
in misty distance—Ulysses addressing
the assembly before the tents, or Achilles
in his golden helmet, racing his chariot
over the sands."

The Frankish king remembered then
an ancient poem recited at his table
by a wandering bard. He'd sung of these things,
astounding the vassals, who plied him with wine
and made him harp those ballads till dawn.

She continued,
"I remember, I was painted and perfumed
and set out on the street for the pleasure of anyone,
however he wanted, for a handful of coins.
I ended up in a tavern, playing a zither
for drunken sailors. A sudden storm
made the roof resound with heavy rain,
high wind blew out the candles. A brawl began.
Fists were swung and curses hurled.
I crouched in a corner and wept for terror.
Someone came in and took me by the hand."

"That was me. I found her where the dregs and jetsam
of a great port collect. I took her with me,
poor little creature, wee being of the pit,
wicked and innocent, virgin and whore.
Simon Magus and the Gnostics called her Ennoia,
Barbelos, and Prounikos: the fallen female
aspect of God. The ancient Greeks
knew her as Eros. In Tyre and Sidon
she was worshipped as Astarte.
Homer and Stesichorus
called her Helen of Troy, the curse
and scourge of Hellas' heroes, the death
of her fancy-man Paris.

"At Rome a plebeian yanked her head back
by the hair and slit her throat
because she'd made him love her just for fun.
Prince Tarquin raped her: she was Lucrece,
and also that Delilah who shaved Samson's head,
the new bride who slew besotted old Attila
on a wedding bed of furs in a tent made of hides

while his dogs howled outside. She was Judith
who hoisted Holofernes' severed head,
nor was he the last man she butchered like a steer.

"Liar, infidel, prostitute,
where didn't she go relentless after pleasure?
She plied her trade in taverns, in alleys.
In Syria she was queen of the thieves,
delightedly they drank their winnings with her.
More than one holy priest shared her bed
still warm from the last man to lie there. I
ransomed her from the guild of thieves,
paid heavily in gold for her well-fed flesh
and pink health. I set her up as a courtesan.
Noble youths, old misers, those who wore jewels
and those who hoarded them followed us around
with desperate looks, holding out crammed purses.

"Nero was obsessed with her,
so much so that he had her killed
lest he fall in love. Caligula
had her poisoned. She was exiled by Titus.
The people adored her pale and perfect face,
they thought she must be the goddess of the moon.

"This is what I do. I bring her to kings,
to any man with real power. All that crimes
of passion or anger can accomplish, comes with her.
There isn't a throne she's approached
that wasn't stained by the shedding of blood
or the spurting of seed. This is my victory,
this is my goal. To destroy everything."

The Frankish king was distressed by this confession,
though not in quite the way one might expect.
There dawned in his soul, and rose
with a more than solar fire, the longing
to take his turn with this woman, the body
he'd glimpsed through her rags, the bruised arms
of a helpless girl, the sleepy-stupid eyes
in her dazed pained face, her verge-of-tears smile,
inflamed him strangely. He wanted to degrade her
for days, to wallow as he wanted
in his dirtiest dreams. He slid off one thick gold
arm-band and passed it to the old man, who gravely
accepted it. The king, with dry mouth and shining eyes,
said, "Bring her to my palace tonight.
My serf will meet you at the gate."

The king's weary retinue followed him home
on the road between the wheat-fields, glad
to be moving on at last. The horses, taken from their grazing,
walked on, no longer interested in anything.

That night, after three jugs of mead
and two of red wine, the king called in his man
Hildebert, explained the situation
which seemed to amuse the serf, for he smiled
as he headed for the gate.

Just then a man leading a pale young girl
took off his sandal and struck the great door
thrice with the flat of it. The heavy portal,
all big iron nail-heads and curlicued hinges,
opened noiselessly. The man at the gate
shoved the girl inside with a mirthless laugh.
That's how the woman whom history knows

as Fredegond found her way into the bedroom
of the Merovingian kings. With her came war,
hatred between Christian peoples,
the dagger, poison and adultery—
all found a home beneath those gothic vaults.

Fredegond stood there with crossed arms, heard
with satisfaction the eager footsteps
of the approaching king. Contented, she foresaw
the crime and disaster soon to be,
from the murder of Audovere
to the final doom inherited
by the last of Chilperic's line,
and her eyes blazed with joy.

LOVE LEFT

for Theodore de Banville

I lay at your door these roses red as blood,
these lilies pale as I've become for love;
their sweet, funereal perfume
enshrouds my soul. You smile
ironically. You're robed in white
like a classical statue of the cruelest god,
Eros. Love refuses.

I caught two doves in the woods, a gift
for you. A little string's enough
to take away their liberty—
your touch has done as much for me.
My heart beats like a frightened bird's.
One kiss, and I'd regain the skies.
Knowing this, Love, evil thing,
Love laughs.

I've brought the riches of the East
for you, things carved from sandalwood,
incense worthy of the gods,
perfume in precious crystal flasks
whose scent's enough to half embalm
one's soul—
Love hesitates.

I've brought you richly woven clothes,
costly cosmetics, spices, jewels.
You glance at these, regard the glare
of all my shiny treasures, then
Love speaks.

No, keep the bracelets, keep the rings,
the suffocating rich perfumes,
and keep your miser heart, I've had
enough. My love has died of your
bought kisses. Love—
Love shudders,

Shut the wicker birdcage well
upon those doves, or let them out
on golden leashes—all in vain,
for Love has fled its gorgeous jail.
Love left.

THE GODS

for Paul de Saint-Victor[41]

Perfumed, tipsy with ambrosia,
halos on their brows,
the gods of Greece and of the east,
these proud, seductive deities,

they dream cruel dreams
of murder and control;
their power is a frenzy
that only crime can calm.

They don't care about the agony
of a world that hates them,
or about the scorn of atheists—
these strong, beautiful gods!

The power of injustice, the power
to bring humanity to its knees
to groan its last—the awful force
that doesn't care who wields it, shines
in their calm, sweet, stupid faces.

Their nakedness is dazzling
and cold as that of the sparkling stars.
They are the silver dream of Time:
Time's longing for eternity.

EROS

Standing in the lightning-white brightness
of a mountain peak that looks down on clouds,
Eros shines, the murderous god.
His firework arrows light up the abyss
that is the human heart.

He sends an arrow hissing up to heaven,
and out of the cruel indifferent blue
falls a scarlet drop to spatter its asterisk
at the naked feet of Eros,
a red and terrible flower that shows another god
has succumbed to some criminal love.

With a splendid sneer this cruellest of archers
slowly bends his ferocious bow,
the arrow flies with an insistent whisper

and down on earth, where every sun must set,
love immortal dawns.

SELENE

Shining white in the darkness
with a gleam like snowy ground on a winter's night,
blond Selene, unveiled, disrobed of cloud,
leads, as in a dream, the ballet of the stars
across the vast black.

Her skin has the milky shimmer of an opal.
there's a slender silver crescent in her pale gold hair,
Smiling, she bends her ebony bow,
which is night itself.

Selene, mother of legends and visions,
of figures that dance, half-glimpsed, in the mist!

Reclining on a cloud, she smiles for the shepherd
on his hillside, for the fisher on the shore,
and all she touches turns to silver.

ZEUS

With eyes closed and halo'd brow,
Zeus, deaf to the weak, attentive to the strong,
maintains the implacable balance of existence
from his brilliant, echoing heavens.

He foresees each effect for he knows every cause,
he gravely contemplates the birth of every age
and, depending on how morose is his mood,
he makes the eras glitter like stars
or darkens them with blood.

He harkens to the sobs, the cries, the death-rattles
rising like incense towards his clouds;
to him, they're sweet as kisses given in a garden.

All Olympus listens, enraptured, to this music,
the true poetry of the ancient world,
the harmonies of hatred, the resonance of pain.

APHRODITE

A team of dolphins pulls her chariot
across the waves. The goddess, mean and treacherous,
shakes her mane, scattering across humankind,
with divine indifference, pearls and drops of blood.

Her only clothing is her long red hair,
as wild as herself. It reaches to her thighs;
through it one might glimpse
a glimmer of bosom, a hint
of mysteries more profound.

In the giggling of children who play forbidden games,
in the screams of cats in heat, her laughter
echoes through the world—

she laughs, allowing us to see her teeth,
so white, so unexpectedly sharp.

APOLLO

Rearing horses draw his red-gold chariot
past mountain peaks into open sky;
Aurora holds the reins, Apollo rides
in dreadful splendor, almost monstrous
in his beauty.

With his hair in the wind, his deep blue eyes
drink in the azure deep; there's nothing he doesn't see.
Poet of the gods, he holds a great harp
in his bare arms. Smiling, he sings.

Eagles circle over his head
crying a chorus to his wild notes.

On earth, mortal singers look up in awe,
eager to be inspired by his lyre
or, at least, to be consumed by his fire.

EPILOGUE

for Gustave Moreau[42]

I

The poet is dead. His carven lyre
floats down the river along with his corpse.
The muse, in tears, holds his severed head
still dripping blood like a butchered beast.

With her fingertips she closes his eyes,
she kisses his white forehead, smooths his hair.
Her pain's as pure as that of an injured animal.

"Farewell," she says. "O poet wanderer,
enchanter of nature, escorted by wolves
and mountain lions tamed by your music.

"Nevermore will inspiration fill this head,
nevermore will song fill this mouth,
nevermore will your magic intoxicate the world."

II

"You marched through the forest
in triumph and rapture,
I led you down each valley and up every hill.

My inspiration filled the sails of your soul.
I flew with you, poet of nature,
with you I forgot the noise of war trumpets,
the metal music of heroic swords.

"You were the poet of a world still young,
still wild. Nymphs of cave and grove
were your retinue. I shared with you the transports
of those who watch the dawn from a mountain peak.

"Now your beautiful body bleeds
to the whiteness of a statue."

Oh, sight of woe!
The muse, like a fairy, in her robe of blue
and bracelets of gold, holds the bloody head
of the demigod. All alone in the depths
of the wood, she weeps for Orpheus.

NOTES

1 Leconte de Lisle (1818-1894) was a poet whose work bridged the Romantic and Symbolist periods in French literature, without involvement in the intervening period of Naturalism. His many translations from ancient Greek made him a particularly fitting recipient for this book, which contains so many classically themed poems.

2 This title alludes to the thirteenth century book *Legenda Aurea*, an encyclopedia of legendary lives of the saints, which was the most popular of its kind in the Middle Ages, and remains a valuable resource for art historians and historians of religion.

3 There is a seventh century Saint Odile of Alsace who, born blind, was able to see after she was baptized at age twelve by St. Erhard of Regensburg. Lorrain's interest in the historical figure was limited to her euphonious name, the legend he tells is of his own devising.

4 This poem is based on "The Marriage of Geraint" in Tennyson's *Idylls of the King*. In that poem Geraint, a knight of Arthur's court, falls in love with Enid, a girl of noble but impoverished family.

5 According to the legend which Tennyson memorably retells in "Merlin and Vivien," the artful Vivien seduces Merlin to

steal from him the secrets of sorcery, which she then uses to imprison him in an endless enchanted sleep.

6 Based on Tennyson's "Lancelot and Elaine." Elaine, daughter of the lord of Castle Shallot, falls in love with Lancelot when he stays there overnight, on a quest. The old story, of one who loves and one who wishes to be no more than a friend, ends fatally.

7 In medieval legend, Melusine was a winged serpent who assumed human form to marry a mortal—a union which ended when, contrary to his promise, her husband spied on her and saw her resume her true shape. Lorrain's version of the story makes her fatal beauty the tale's sole focus.

8 Witlaw is not a specific king. The geography and genealogy here, which may exasperate the serious medievalist, were meant only to evoke the mood of the European Dark Ages as imagined by the Romantics.

9 Though we think of Victor Hugo as a novelist, in France he is also remembered as a great and prolific poet. His work in verse has, regrettably, not yet found an adequate translator into English.

10 Theodore de Banville was at this time considered one of the great poets of Baudelaire's generation.

11 Briseis was a princess from Lyrnessa, a city-state in Asia Minor, a little south of Troy. When the Greeks conquered Lyrnessa as part of their Trojan campaign, the captive Briseis was given to Achilles as a prize. Agamemnon took her from Achilles, initiating the events described in the Iliad.

12 In Greek mythology, Andromeda is the daughter of an Ethiopian king. When a sea-monster ravaged her country's coast, Andromeda was offered to it, a victim to placate the angry gods. She was rescued by Perseus, the hero who slew Medusa and tamed Pegasus.

13 Andromache was the wife of the Trojan prince Hector. After Troy's fall, she became the slave of Achilles' son Pyrrhus. Pyrrhus would kill Andromache's son Astyanax by throwing him from the walls of captured Troy, lest he grow up to avenge his father, Hector, whom Achilles had slain.

14 Simon Magus was a Gnostic competitor with St. Paul in the salvation trade. He claimed Ennoia, (in Gnostic myth, the fallen female aspect of God), had suffered many and progressively more degraded incarnations, one of which was Helen of Troy, and that he, Simon, had discovered her working in a brothel, and made her his consort. Thus, Simon claimed, he had effectually married into the Divine Family, and in a manner that justified his teaching that mystical attainment could be gained through debauchery.

15 Cassandra was a Trojan princess, gifted with prophecy, but cursed to never have her warnings believed. After Troy's fall, she became the slave and concubine of Agamemnon, with whom she was finally slain by Agamemnon's wife, Clytemnestra.

16 This is based on Goethe's 1744 poem *The King of Thule*, which Goethe would use in *Faust, Part One* (lines 2759-82), as a song sung by Gretchen, foreshadowing her tragic love for Faust. In Goethe's poem the king cherishes a golden cup, the final gift from his deceased wife. At the end of his life, after he has bequeathed all his other possessions to his son,

he throws the cup into the sea, signifying his acceptance of death and the endurance of his love. A French version of the poem, set to music by Jean Baptiste Wecherlin (1821-1910), was published in 1880, two years before *Blood of the Gods* was published. The dedication to Judith Gautier is significant. As a youth, Lorrain (b. 1855) had a crush on Judith Gautier (b. 1845), eldest daughter of Theophile Gautier, the poet to whom Baudelaire dedicated *The Flowers of Evil*. A brilliant young woman, at the age of eighteen she made her reputation with *The Jade Book*, a collection of translations from the Chinese. She was the friend of Flaubert, Victor Hugo and Wagner. Judith appreciated the adolescent Lorrain's precocity, but she was a decade older than him, married to the poet Catulle Mendes, and she was aware, if he was not, that he was gay—so this friendship could not develop into a reciprocated romance. Lorrain would later claim that this early disappointment in love had turned him from women. Perhaps he had in mind the tradition, which Ovid repeats in his *Metamorphoses*, that Orpheus devoted himself exclusively to boys after losing Eurydice. Too, Lorrain's medievalism favored the pose of the courtly lover forever faithful to his unattainable lady.

17 As the dedication to this poignant poem would suggest, Lorrain was devoted to his mother. He more or less lived with her all his life.

18 Though the lady is otherwise unknown, the family name de Bonis is ancient and noble in Italy and can be traced back to thirteenth-century Milan.

19 Apollonia is the name of a famous ancient Greek city on the coast of what is now Albania. The Marquise of Héricourt is otherwise unknown. In all likelihood her first name was Apollonia and she had a taste for classical antiquity, and that sufficed to inspire this poem.

20 The right of a feudal lord to enjoy the wedding night with the bride of his newly-married subject is attested as far back as the fourteenth century in poetry. It became a well-known literary theme in the eighteenth century, though this was due more to a desire to denigrate the expiring remnants of feudalism than to the existence, then or ever, of the phenomenon as a social reality. As such, the custom is a plot element in Beaumarchais' *The Marriage of Figaro*.

21 This Latin tag is from Virgil's *Aeneid*, 1: 462, and means "the nature of existence is sorrowful."

22 Lorrain was keenly aware of his mother's marital unhappiness, for which he was her principal consolation. Living in a dull provincial town, her husband was a practical businessman, twenty years older than she, below her station in culture, and at times unfaithful.

23 Madame Heuzé, the dedicatee, is otherwise unknown.

24 This fantasy in the medieval Celtic style is entirely the product of Lorrain's imagination and bears no relation to *Harold*, Tennyson's 1876 historical drama. The dedication simply expresses Lorrain's admiration for Tennyson's many outstanding poems on Celtic legendary themes.

25 Jean Richepin (1849-1926), a friend of Artur Rimbaud, made his name with his 1876 *The Song of the Poor*, a slangy tour of low life and poverty in the spirit of Francois Villon—a book which cost him an obscenity trial and a month in prison.

26 Prudhomme (1839-1907) was a highly regarded sentimental poet who received the Nobel Prize for Literature in 1901.

27 Jean Gounod (1856-1935) was the son of the French composer Charles-François Gounod, who is best remembered for his *Ave Maria* and his opera *Faust*.

28 This dedicatee is otherwise unknown.

29 The dedicatee of this and the following poem, Armand Silvestre, was a minor poet and art critic. As for the Cardinal of Ragusa, Andrea Foscari, the king of Parma and the Duke of Ferrara, Lorrain has taken names from Renaissance history for their poetic color, with no particular regard for real persons or events.

30 It is unclear whom Lorrain intended with this dedication. Goethe, who wrote dramas about both Faust and Romeo, seems possible.

31 There is no such poem as Lorrain alludes to by Tennyson.

32 Addressing this poem to Gustave Flaubert, Lorrain wasn't thinking of the author of *Madame Bovary*, but of *Salaambo*, a fabulously over-wrought re-creation of ancient Carthage. In Greek, "ephebe" means a young man between eighteen and twenty.

33 Ganymede was a young Trojan prince whom Zeus, in the form of an eagle, kidnapped to Olympus, where he became the god's cup-bearer and submissive boy.

34 Hylas was the young boyfriend of Hercules; he was kidnapped by amorous nymphs as he drew water from their fountain.

35 Bathyllus was a dancer and actor in Nero's Rome, famed for his comic genius and especially his erotic dancing.

36 Attis was a folklore figure from classical antiquity who castrated himself as an act of devotion to Cybele, a mother goddess from Asia Minor.

37 Patroclus was Achilles's boyfriend. The *Iliad* is essentially the story of how this bereft hero avenged Patroculus' death.

38 Antinous was a teenage boy from Asia Minor who became the favorite and lover of the fifty-something Roman emperor Hadrian in the early second century CE. Antinous accidentally drowned in the Nile in the year 130.

39 Princess Audovere was a sixth-century Frankish queen, first wife of Chilperic I, the hero of the following poem. In this poem we have a portrait of young Audovere before her marriage.

40 Ennoia, a figure from gnostic mythology, was introduced above in the *Golden Legends* section. We need only add that Chilperic I was the sixth century king of the western part of the Frankish realm, and he spent his life fighting with his brothers for dominion over the whole. Audovere was his first wife. The slave woman Fredegonde displaced her, and greatly accelerated Chilperic's progress through the extremes of brutality, treachery and piety that were the norm among the recently and superficially Christianized Germanic barbarians. Chiliperic's reputation is particularly black since he made a personal enemy of Geoffrey of Tours, whose *History of the Franks* is our primary source for this period in French history.

41 Paul de Saint-Victor was a minor essayist and literary critic.

42 Gustave Moreau was a reclusive older homosexual painter whose friendship Lorrain won by unfeigned admiration. Though Moreau was reasonably successful, Huysman's ecstatic approbation of his Salome paintings, voiced by des Esseintes in the novel *À rebours*, made Moreau a culture hero. Though Moreau's place in the pantheon of Symbolist painters is central and secure, his genius is more generally appreciated today in his illustrations for La Fontaine's *Fables*.

A PARTIAL LIST OF SNUGGLY BOOKS

G. ALBERT AURIER *Elsewhere and Other Stories*
CHARLES BARBARA *My Lunatic Asylum*
CHARLES BARBARA *Stirring Stories*
S. HEZOLNRY BERTHOUD *Misanthropic Tales*
LÉON BLOY *The Tarantulas' Parlor and Other Unkind Tales*
ÉLÉMIR BOURGES *The Twilight of the Gods*
ADA BUISSON *The Baron's Coffin and Other Disquieting Tales*
CYRIEL BUYSSE *The Aunts*
JAMES CHAMPAGNE *Harlem Smoke*
FÉLICIEN CHAMPSAUR *The Latin Orgy*
ARMAND CHARPENTIER
   Claustrophobic Madness and Other Stories of Death and Love
BRENDAN CONNELL *Metrophilias*
BRENDAN CONNELL *Spells*
RENDAN CONNELL (editor) *The Zaffre Book of Occult Fiction*
BRENDAN CONNELL (editor) *The Zinzolin Book of Occult Fiction*
RAFAELA CONTRERAS *The Turquoise Ring and Other Stories*
DANIEL CORRICK (editor)
   Ghosts and Robbers: An Anthology of German Gothic Fiction
ADOLFO COUVE *When I Think of My Missing Head*
RENÉ CREVEL *Are You All Crazy?*
QUENTIN S. CRISP *Aiaigasa*
QUENTIN S. CRISP *Rule Dementia!*
LUCIE DELARUE-MARDRUS *The Last Siren and Other Stories*
LADY DILKE *The Outcast Spirit and Other Stories*
CATHERINE DOUSTEYSSIER-KHOZE *The Beauty of the Death Cap*
ÉDOUARD DUJARDIN *Hauntings*
BERIT ELLINGSEN *Now We Can See the Moon*
ERCKMANN-CHATRIAN *A Malediction*
ALPHONSE ESQUIROS *The Enchanted Castle*
ENRIQUE GÓMEZ CARRILLO *Sentimental Stories*
DELPHI FABRICE *Flowers of Ether*
DELPHI FABRICE *The Red Sorcerer*
DELPHI FABRICE *The Red Spider*
BENJAMIN GASTINEAU *The Reign of Satan*
EDMOND AND JULES DE GONCOURT *Manette Salomon*
REMY DE GOURMONT *From a Faraway Land*
REMY DE GOURMONT *Morose Vignettes*
GUIDO GOZZANO *Alcina and Other Stories*
GUSTAVE GUICHES *The Modesty of Sodom*
EDWARD HERON-ALLEN *The Complete Shorter Fiction*
EDWARD HERON-ALLEN *Three Ghost-Written Novels*

J.-K. HUYSMANS *The Crowds of Lourdes*
J.-K. HUYSMANS *Knapsacks*
COLIN INSOLE *Valerie and Other Stories*
JUSTIN ISIS *Pleasant Tales II*
JULES JANIN *The Dead Donkey and the Guillotined Woman*
VICTOR JOLY *The Unknown Collaborator and Other Legendary Tales*
GUSTAVE KAHN *The Mad King*
MARIE KRYSINSKA *The Path of Amour*
BERNARD LAZARE *The Mirror of Legends*
BERNARD LAZARE *The Torch-Bearers*
MAURICE LEVEL *The Shadow*
JEAN LORRAIN *Errant Vice*
JEAN LORRAIN *Fards and Poisons*
JEAN LORRAIN *Masks in the Tapestry*
JEAN LORRAIN *Monsieur de Bougrelon and Other Stories*
JEAN LORRAIN *Nightmares of an Ether-Drinker*
JEAN LORRAIN *The Soul-Drinker and Other Decadent Fantasies*
GEORGES DE LYS *An Idyll in Sodom*
GEORGES DE LYS *Penthesilea*
ARTHUR MACHEN *N*
ARTHUR MACHEN *Ornaments in Jade*
CAMILLE MAUCLAIR *The Frail Soul and Other Stories*
CATULLE MENDÈS *Bluebirds*
CATULLE MENDÈS *For Reading in the Bath*
CATULLE MENDÈS *Mephistophela*
ÉPHRAÏM MIKHAËL *Halyartes and Other Poems in Prose*
LUIS DE MIRANDA *Who Killed the Poet?*
OCTAVE MIRBEAU *The Death of Balzac*
CHARLES MORICE *Babels, Balloons and Innocent Eyes*
GABRIEL MOUREY *Monada*
DAMIAN MURPHY *Daughters of Apostasy*
KRISTINE ONG MUSLIM *Butterfly Dream*
OSSIT *Ilse*
CHARLES NODIER *Outlaws and Sorrows*
HERSH DOVID NOMBERG *A Cheerful Soul and Other Stories*
PHILOTHÉE O'NEDDY *The Enchanted Ring*
GEORGES DE PEYREBRUNE *A Decadent Woman*
HÉLÈNE PICARD *Sabbat*
URSULA PFLUG *Down From*
JEAN PRINTEMPS *Whimsical Tales*
JEREMY REED *When a Girl Loves a Girl*
ADOLPHE RETTÉ *Misty Thule*
JEAN RICHEPIN *The Bull-Man and the Grasshopper*
FREDERICK ROLFE (Baron Corvo) *Amico di Sandro*
FREDERICK ROLFE (Baron Corvo) *An Ossuary of the North Lagoon and Other Stories*

JASON ROLFE *An Archive of Human Nonsense*
ARNAUD RYKNER *The Last Train*
LEOPOLD VON SACHER-MASOCH *The Black Gondola and Other Stories*
MARCEL SCHWOB *The Assassins and Other Stories*
MARCEL SCHWOB *Double Heart*
CHRISTIAN HEINRICH SPIESS *The Dwarf of Westerbourg*
BRIAN STABLEFORD (editor) *The Alabaster Book of Occult Fiction*
BRIAN STABLEFORD (editor)
    Decadence and Symbolism: A Showcase Anthology
BRIAN STABLEFORD (editor) *The Snuggly Satyricon*
BRIAN STABLEFORD (editor) *The Snuggly Satanicon*
BRIAN STABLEFORD (editor) *The Vermilion Book of Occult Fiction*
BRIAN STABLEFORD *Spirits of the Vasty Deep*
COUNT ERIC STENBOCK *Love, Sleep & Dreams*
COUNT ERIC STENBOCK *Myrtle, Rue & Cypress*
COUNT ERIC STENBOCK *The Shadow of Death*
COUNT ERIC STENBOCK *Studies of Death*
MONTAGUE SUMMERS *The Bride of Christ and Other Fictions*
MONTAGUE SUMMERS *Six Ghost Stories*
ALICE TÉLOT *The Inn of Tears*
GILBERT-AUGUSTIN THIERRY *The Blonde Tress and The Mask*
GILBERT-AUGUSTIN THIERRY *Reincarnation and Redemption*
DOUGLAS THOMPSON *The Fallen West*
TOADHOUSE *Gone Fishing with Samy Rosenstock*
TOADHOUSE *Living and Dying in a Mind Field*
TOADHOUSE *What Makes the Wave Break?*
LÉO TRÉZENIK *The Confession of a Madman*
LÉO TRÉZENIK *Decadent Prose Pieces*
RUGGERO VASARI *Raun*
JANE DE LA VAUDÈRE *The Demi-Sexes and The Androgynes*
JANE DE LA VAUDÈRE *The Double Star and Other Occult Fantasies*
JANE DE LA VAUDÈRE *The Mystery of Kama and Brahma's Courtesans*
JANE DE LA VAUDÈRE *Three Flowers and The King of Siam's Amazon*
JANE DE LA VAUDÈRE *The Witch of Ecbatana and The Virgin of Israel*
AUGUSTE VILLIERS DE L'ISLE-ADAM *Isis*
RENÉE VIVIEN AND HÉLÈNE DE ZUYLEN DE NYEVELT
    Faustina and Other Stories
RENÉE VIVIEN *Lilith's Legacy*
RENÉE VIVIEN *A Woman Appeared to Me*
ILARIE VORONCA *The Confession of a False Soul*
ILARIE VORONCA *The Key to Reality*
TERESA WILMS MONTT *In the Stillness of Marble*
TERESA WILMS MONTT *Sentimental Doubts*
KAREL VAN DE WOESTIJNE *The Dying Peasant*

www.ingramcontent.com/pod-product-compliance
Lightning Source LLC
Chambersburg PA
CBHW020535080526
44583CB00013B/867